the easy dinner cookbook

the easy dinner cookbook

no-fuss recipes for family-friendly meals

by chef emery

photography by biz jones

ROCKRIDGE
PRESS

This cookbook is dedicated to my beautiful family, Troy, Elliott, and Arabella, who inspire me every day to cook wholesome, delicious meals.

Contents

CHAPTER 6 **Slow Cooker & Pressure Cooker** 75

CHAPTER 7 **Simple Sides** 93

Introduction

"What's for Dinner?"

The ever-present question. In many circumstances, asking what's for dinner induces excitement and joy; in others, the question amounts to a challenge—particularly for busy people trying to put good food on the table for themselves and their families without emptying their wallets.

As a business owner, mother, and chef, I'm all too familiar with both responses. Although most of us can agree that we *want* to eat something nourishing, healthy, fresh, and relatively inexpensive, turning that prospect into a reality can be hard at times. There are obstacles nearly everyone faces—including me. Maybe you didn't have time to pick up the perfect ingredients from the grocery store. Maybe you forgot to defrost a piece of meat in the morning before you left for work. Maybe your daughter wants something different than your spouse. Maybe you're just exhausted! Whatever the case may be, getting a delicious, satisfying meal on the table is not always as easy as it sounds.

This common struggle is why I'm so excited to share *The Easy Dinner Cookbook* with you. In the opening chapter, I provide some helpful time-saving tips, equipment lists, and grocery-shopping suggestions, as well as practical advice on making the most of your freezer and leftovers. Once you've created a stress-free kitchen, you can use this book's recipes to make easy yet flavorful meals—from Spice-Rubbed Pork Tenderloin (see page 73) to Easy Chicken Cacciatore (see page 58)—for your whole family to enjoy.

Almost all of the recipes serve four to six people, though they can be modified for more or fewer. Each recipe in chapters 2 through 6 should be considered an entrée. Helpful tips make preparing your dinner as seamless as possible.

This cookbook relies heavily on whole foods and natural ingredients; you'll never be in doubt about a recipe's contents, thanks to dietary labels and nutritional information accompanying each recipe. Many dishes, I'm happy to say, can be completed in under 30 minutes. And if you're looking to fill your dinner table with delicious sides, I've provided 10 of my favorites in chapter 7, all of which can be prepared in a few simple steps.

Ultimately, my hope is this book will alleviate some of the stress that comes with making a great-tasting dinner, so you can focus on what really matters: gathering your family and friends together to enjoy a meal.

CHAPTER 1

Dinner Made Easy

Making a home-cooked dinner for your family can feel like a daunting task. Think of this opening chapter as a one-stop shop full of the resources and know-how to efficiently put together a delicious meal. I've included meal planning basics, shopping tips, the best ways to stock your kitchen, and much more, to make cooking great food as easy as possible. The goal? Less time worrying about dinner and more time enjoying your meal with the people you love most. Let's get started!

‹ Miso Sheet Pan Salmon, page 63
Cilantro Lime Rice, page 101

The Joys of a Home-Cooked Dinner

Dinner with family and friends can be one of the most powerful ways of connecting. Even if just for 20 minutes, taking time out of our busy days to enjoy a meal without distractions can reduce stress and help us communicate with those who are most important to us. In a fast-paced culture, the home-cooked dinner can serve as a kind of balm—a modest, yet significant, form of self-care, fruitful for the mind, body, and soul. The simple act of preparing a meal and eating together is an easy, timeless way to show the people in our lives how much we value them.

And yet, this simple act is increasingly under threat. According to the Economic Research Service's *Adult Eating & Health Module* report, during the last 10 years, Americans have spent increasingly less time eating meals and gathering for family dinners. Another study, published in the *Journal of Experimental Social Psychology*, found that using smartphones while we eat can diminish our enjoyment of the meal. The *Washington Post* reported that "the presence of mobile technologies has the potential to divert individuals from face-to-face exchanges, thereby undermining the character and depth of these connections."

Don't get me wrong: Smartphones have their time and place—so do store-bought packaged meals, our favorite delivery items, and, of course, nights out at restaurants. I understand that your time is precious and that you may not be able to make dinner every night. But I promise you, doing so will be worth the effort! No one ever looks back and regrets taking the time to sit down with family and friends to enjoy a home-cooked feast.

Using Daylight

We all lead busy lives, and finding the time to prepare dinner can be a challenge. Here are some time-saving tips:

- Thaw meats by placing them in a container in the refrigerator before leaving home for the day.

- Place your rice in a rice cooker (a great investment) and set it in the morning.

- Wash and cut veggies in advance per the recipe you plan to cook; you can even place them in a steamer or lay them out on a sheet pan.

- Mince garlic, ginger, or fresh herbs and store them covered in the refrigerator.

- Set the dinner table the night before or in the morning.

- Whenever you have the time, make a salad and store it covered in the refrigerator.

Dinner, the French Way

According to recent figures from the Organisation for Economic Co-operation and Development (OECD), the French, on average, spend more than twice as long eating per day than Americans, a phenomenon attributable to France's relatively long lunch break and to dinnertime traditions, which can include an aperitif (a predinner cocktail hour for drinks and nibbles), followed by several courses and dessert, followed by a digestif (an after-dinner drink, like cognac). Culturally, the French make lingering over a meal a priority, in a way Americans, by and large, do not.

I am not saying we should spend two hours at the table every night. But let France's appreciation for dinner inspire you to take yours more seriously. Add an aperitif to your schedule every so often!

Creating a Stress-Free Kitchen

Creating a stress-free kitchen will help you get dinner on the table with relatively little effort. Use separate drawers to organize kitchen tools and utensils and baskets to organize your pantry dry goods. I love placing a cake stand right next to my stovetop for all my essentials, like olive oil, sea salt, black pepper, and garlic.

The Equipment

I've created two lists of kitchen tools and utensils. The first includes those you'll need to make the recipes in this book; the second includes nice-to-have tools that will help you cook more efficiently.

Need to Have

- Can opener
- Chef's knife (I recommend Wüsthof)
- Colander
- Cutting board
- Loaf pan
- Measuring cups and spoons
- Mixing bowls
- Oven mitts
- Rubber spatulas
- Saucepans or pots with lids
- Sheet pans
- Stainless steel or cast iron skillet (preferably 12-inch)
- Three-quart baking or casserole dish
- Vegetable peeler
- Wooden spoons

Nice to Have

Electric pressure cooker or slow cooker These are great pieces of kitchenware to invest in, if you want to practice true "set it and forget it" cooking—and eat delicious food as a result. Chapter 6 is entirely devoted to pressure cooker and slow cooker recipes; although the instructions work regardless of the brand, I personally use an Instant Pot (for my pressure cooker) and a Crock-Pot (for my slow cooker).

Food processor Every home chef should invest in a food processor, which chops, dices, and emulsifies foods quickly and easily.

Freezer-friendly bags A great option for keeping your leftovers and meals organized, freezer-friendly bags are smaller than other containers but often hold up to a gallon or more. These bags can be labeled with the date and recipe title for easier management of your meals. Also, placing the bags on a flat surface while they're freezing will allow you to stack them once they're frozen solid, and help save space.

Garlic press Use this tool to quickly press or mince garlic.

Glass food storage containers I prefer these for storing leftovers in the refrigerator, as well as for meal prep. Food placed in the refrigerator will last almost twice as long in an airtight glass container than in a bowl or on a plate.

Handheld lemon squeezer This tool is inexpensive, quick to clean, and makes juicing effortless.

Immersion blender This is another really great piece of kitchen equipment. It emulsifies (combines) soups quickly, and is perfect for making smoothies, guacamole, pesto, and so much more.

Instant-read thermometer If you're new to cooking, this tool is especially helpful. Standard internal temperatures are: 165°F for chicken and turkey, 145°F for beef (cooked to medium-well), and 160°F for pork and ground beef.

Kitchen scissors I always like to have a good pair of kitchen scissors on hand to quickly open things and trim certain meats.

Ladle A good ladle makes serving chilies, curries, soups, and stews a breeze.

Microplane This inexpensive tool zests lemons and spices quickly with minimal cleanup.

Salad spinner You'll use this tool to wash and dry your salad greens without getting them soggy. Taking away the extra moisture will also keep your greens fresh longer.

Tongs Grab a pair of tongs to flip your meat and vegetables in the pan or oven.

Rice cooker This reasonably priced kitchen gadget is great for making steamed rice. You can set it and forget it on busy days.

If You Don't Have an Electric Pressure Cooker or Slow Cooker . . . Read This

Chapter 6 is devoted to recipes that call for a slow cooker or pressure cooker. The slow cooker is a large electric pot used for cooking food slowly (as the name suggests) in order to tenderize and infuse it with flavor. A pressure cooker accomplishes these same tasks, while saving energy, by expelling air and trapping steam produced from the boiling liquid inside. This airtight electric pot quickly cooks meats, pastas and rice, vegetables, and, particularly, stews.

The slow cooker and pressure cooker save a tremendous amount of time and effort: If you do not have a slow cooker or pressure cooker, you can use a cast iron pot with a lid or an oven-safe pot with a lid to slow cook recipes in the oven at 350°F for two to three hours. Alternatively, depending on the recipe, you can use a saucepan or skillet with a lid to do these recipes on your stovetop on low heat for several hours.

The Pantry

A well-stocked and organized pantry is essential to stress-free cooking. When we have what we need on hand, we can bring great-tasting meals together quickly and easily.

Need to Have

Almost all this book's recipes use one or more of these four basic pantry staples: salt, black pepper, oil, and vinegar. I recommend using a good quality sea salt, like Maldon, and freshly ground black pepper; you'll taste the difference in your meals. Vinegars are a wonderful staple for cooking—I personally love Bragg Apple Cider Vinegar—and investing in high-quality extra-virgin olive oil is worth the cost.

Nice to Have

Here are some additional pantry staples that are great to have on hand.

- Baking powder
- Baking soda
- Balsamic vinegar
- Barbecue sauce
- Bay leaves (for soups and stews)
- Beans

- Chili powder
- Cinnamon
- Curry powder
- Dried oregano
- Dried pasta
- Dried thyme

- Ground cumin
- Honey
- Marinara sauce
- Rice (basmati, brown, or white)
- Soy sauce

A Wine Pairing Cheat Sheet

In general, red wines, like pinot noirs, merlots, and cabernets, go with heartier, savory meals like red meat dishes, pasta with various red sauces, and stews. White wines, like Riesling, chardonnays, and pinot grigios are perfect in summer and for lighter fare, like fish, salads, and veggie pasta dishes.

Experimenting on your own is part of the fun, but I'll leave you with a few specific recommendations. My Red Wine–Braised Beef (see page 90) and Easy Baked Ziti (see page 69) would work well with a pinot noir or merlot. My Miso Sheet Pan Salmon (see page 63) would pair nicely with a glass of Riesling or chardonnay. Both my Garlic Shrimp Risotto (see page 53) and White Fish with Roasted Tomatoes and Garlic (see page 64) would complement a rosé or pinot grigio.

Making the Most of Your Groceries

Grocery shopping with a plan can save you time and money. The following tips will ensure you don't shop 'til you drop.

- Pick one day of the week to grocery shop.

- Before your trip to the store, write down the recipes that you plan to cook each day of the coming week. When making your selections, consider ingredient lists. The lists for many of this book's recipes overlap, which can reduce both your bill and food wastage.

- Make a grocery list and organize it by fruits, vegetables, meats, and pantry staples, in that exact order, so like items are grouped together. Then shop in that order. Doing so will help you find, bag, unpack, and store your groceries quickly.

- Look for fruits and veggies that are fresh and in season.

- When less perishable items, like canned beans, tomato sauce, rice, or pasta, are on sale, buy them in bulk to save money. You'll end up using them eventually.

- Store your groceries so as to lengthen their shelf life. Pat dry and place all vegetables in the crisper section of your refrigerator. Put all dried goods and pantry items in a cool, dry place. Check expiration dates on all meats and freeze or refrigerate them accordingly.

Making the Most of Your Freezer

When items like bread, fish, shrimp, meat, and frozen fruit and vegetables are on sale, purchase them in bulk and throw them in the freezer. Bagged frozen fruit and veggies will last four to six months in your freezer, and meat, if double-wrapped in plastic wrap, will last two to three months—longer if they're vacuum packed. Freezer wrap is perfect for turkey burgers, salmon fillets, or comparable meat and fish. (I recommend double-wrapping to prevent freezer burn.)

Be sure to label and date the foods you freeze. When buying in bulk, in particular, I also suggest portioning and wrapping your food in individual servings before freezing them to allow you to more easily select and defrost what you're serving on a given night. Lay the bags flat and stack them to save space in your freezer (and to save time retrieving them).

This book's recipes for stews and soups can be doubled, frozen, and defrosted at a later date for a no-stress dinner. Make sure they're fully cooled before putting them in freezer-friendly containers with lids (steer clear of glass for freezing). I do not recommend re-freezing previously thawed foods, because they will lose flavor once thawed again and could get freezer burn.

Freezer-wise, one of my favorite things to do is purchase a full salmon fillet, cut it in half, use one half for dinner that night, and wrap the other in a freezer-friendly bag for another day. If stored in the freezer, fish will generally last a month. You can also freeze leftover sauces, like pesto, to later transform an otherwise lackluster meal into something special.

Making the Most of Your Leftovers

Leftovers are the busy home chef's best friend. So many of the recipes in this book can be easily reheated for next-day lunches or dinners, helping you stretch your dollar, reduce food waste, and manage your meals throughout the week.

To make leftovers last as long as possible in the refrigerator, I recommend using airtight glass containers with lids; meals in this book will last four to five days that way, unless otherwise specified. You can reheat your leftovers and enjoy them as is or find a creative way to use them to make the most out of what you have in your kitchen.

Unless I have a full meal at my disposal, I typically try to pair the previous night's leftovers with fresh ingredients. If I've got leftover Spice-Rubbed Pork Tenderloin (see page 73), for example, I might toss the tenderloin over a bed of fresh spinach or pasta. If I have leftover Fresh Summer Pesto Pasta (see page 33), I might add a fresh protein, like chicken or shrimp, making a smaller portion of the previous night's dinner a bit more substantial.

When in doubt, I rely on a few go-to methods for remixing leftovers. Reheat the stews in chapter 6, for example, and serve them over mashed potatoes or noodles. Use that leftover pesto (see page 33) on zucchini noodles instead of regular pasta for a lighter, lower-carb lunch. Throw your leftover sheet pan meals from chapter 5 in a cast iron skillet (or wok) for an easy, next-day stir-fry. And don't be afraid to use last night's dinner for a savory breakfast. Though a bit unconventional, the Lemon Quinoa Salad (see page 98) tossed in a skillet with a fried egg makes for a quick, satisfactory, and nutritious treat on a weekday morning.

About the Recipes

As you might've gleaned from the table of contents, the chapters in this book are primarily organized by cooking method: No-Cook (recipes require prep but no cooking), 5-Ingredient (recipes require five ingredients or less, excluding salt, black pepper, oil, and vinegar, which are considered staples), One-Pot & Skillet (recipes only require a single pot or skillet to cook), Sheet Pan & Baking Dish (recipes utilize a sheet pan or baking dish), and Slow Cooker & Pressure Cooker (recipes utilize either a slow cooker or an electric pressure cooker).

By and large, the recipes make full meals; those that don't come with recommendations to transform them into full meals (oftentimes with the sides from chapter 7). All of the recipes provide storage instructions for leftovers.

The Labels

The recipes will feature one or more of the following labels.

Dairy-Free The recipe does not contain dairy.

Freezer-Friendly The recipe is easy to freeze and defrost for use at a later date.

Gluten-Free The recipe does not contain gluten. (However, depending on your sensitivity to gluten, you will want to check the labels on packaged or processed ingredients in recipes with this label.)

Vegetarian The recipe does not contain meat or fish.

30-Minute The recipe will take 30 minutes or less to make, from start to finish.

The Tips

All recipes come with at least one of the following tips:

Easy Substitution Suggestions for an easy ingredient swap or variation to help accommodate both seasonality and a variety of flavor preferences.

Lunch Remix Inventive ways to use leftovers from the recipe for lunch the next day.

Make It Faster or Make It Slower If the recipe is for slow cookers, it includes a Make It Faster tip for a pressure cooker adaptation; if the recipe is for pressure cooking, it includes a Make It Slower tip for a slow cooker adaptation.

Pair With A classic one- or two-ingredient side, or a side from chapter 7, is recommended to pair with the recipe.

Troubleshooting This tip helps you avoid common cooking mistakes.

Modifying Serving Sizes

Most recipes in this book serve four to six people, but they can be adjusted for fewer or more. By cutting in half or doubling ingredients accordingly and following the instructions as written, you can tailor these recipes to fit any number of servings. Before you start making a recipe, just take a moment to think about how many servings you'd like.

CHAPTER 2

No-Cook

Let's face it: Some nights, you just don't have the energy to cook, but fatigue shouldn't stop you from enjoying a delicious, freshly prepared dinner in the comfort of your home. From nutritious salads to savory wraps, these "no-cook" recipes may not require much effort to create, but they are destined to become reliable staples.

Refreshing Summer Gazpacho

SERVES
4 TO 6

PREP TIME:
15 MINUTES
PLUS 30
MINUTES TO
REST

DAIRY-FREE

GF

GLUTEN-FREE

VEGETARIAN

Refreshing, light, healthy flavorful—nothing beats a cool gazpacho on a hot day (or a cool day, when you simply don't feel like cooking). Gazpacho is a zesty, tomato-based soup, with finely chopped raw vegetables. Like the essence of the ripest tomato, this cold soup captures sun-drenched summer at its peak. This particular gazpacho is especially tasty when tomatoes and cucumbers are in season.

Juice from ½ lime

Juice from 1 lemon

¼ cup extra-virgin olive oil

½ cup white vinegar

2 tablespoons Worcestershire sauce

2 cups tomato juice

4 large tomatoes, cored and diced

1 garlic clove, minced

2 cucumbers, peeled and chopped

2 red peppers, seeded and chopped

1 tablespoon minced fresh cilantro

1 tablespoon minced fresh parsley

1 tablespoon minced fresh dill

Salt

Freshly ground black pepper

1. In a medium bowl, whisk the lime juice, lemon juice, olive oil, vinegar, Worcestershire sauce, and tomato juice, and set aside.

2. In a large bowl, combine the tomatoes, garlic, cucumbers, red peppers, cilantro, parsley, dill, and tomato juice mixture, and toss to coat evenly.

3. Season with salt and black pepper, then let rest at room temperature for 20 to 30 minutes. This soup will get better as it stands, and is perfect for a next-day lunch or dinner.

4. Serve immediately, or store in an airtight container in the refrigerator up to six days.

Troubleshooting: Make sure to finely chop the vegetables so they are not too chunky—that's key for this recipe!

PER SERVING **CALORIES: 216; SATURATED FAT: 2G; TOTAL FAT: 13G; PROTEIN: 4G; TOTAL CARBS: 23G; FIBER: 4G; SODIUM: 472MG**

Broccoli Salad with Pecans

SERVES
4 TO 6

PREP TIME:
20 MINUTES

DAIRY-FREE

GF

GLUTEN-FREE

VEGETARIAN

30-MINUTE

There are plenty of reasons to love this broccoli salad. It's incredibly versatile—you can omit or add whichever dried fruits, nuts, seeds, and additional veggies you like—and is a fantastic meal to prepare for the week ahead because it gets better the longer it sits in the marinade. It's perfect for picnics, potlucks, and entertaining.

½ cup mayonnaise

½ cup white wine vinegar

3 tablespoons real maple syrup

Juice of 1 lemon

1 teaspoon salt, plus more
   as needed

Dash freshly ground black
   pepper, plus more as needed

2 heads broccoli, stemmed
   and chopped

¼ red onion, diced

½ cup raisins

½ cup sunflower seeds

½ cup pecans

3 to 4 radishes, ends removed
   and sliced (optional)

1. In a large bowl, whisk the mayonnaise, vinegar, maple syrup, lemon juice, salt, and black pepper until fully combined.

2. Add the broccoli, onion, raisins, sunflower seeds, pecans, and radishes (if using) to the bowl and toss thoroughly through the dressing.

3. Season once more with salt and black pepper and serve immediately, or store in an airtight container in the refrigerator up to five days.

Lunch Remix: This recipe is great served the next day for lunch over a bed of salad greens or with the Lemon Quinoa Salad (see page 98).

PER SERVING **CALORIES: 488; SATURATED FAT: 3G; TOTAL FAT: 30G; PROTEIN: 12G; TOTAL CARBS: 51G; FIBER: 9G; SODIUM: 861MG**

Classic Caprese Salad

This classic caprese salad looks as wonderful as it tastes and is especially delicious when tomatoes are at their peak ripeness. The timeless Italian combination of fresh basil, tomatoes, and cheese makes for a refreshing starter to a big meal or a light entrée on its own. Word to the wise: This dish hinges on the quality of the ingredients, so select the freshest you can find!

SERVES
4

PREP TIME:
20 MINUTES

GF

GLUTEN-FREE

VEGETARIAN

30-MINUTE

2 large tomatoes, cored and sliced

2 cups fresh basil leaves

1 (7-ounce) container fresh mozzarella, drained and sliced

Salt

Freshly ground black pepper

½ cup of your favorite vinaigrette

1. On a large plate, layer a slice of tomato, a few leaves of basil, and a slice of mozzarella.

2. Repeat with new layers until you have used all the ingredients.

3. Season with salt and black pepper, then drizzle with vinaigrette before serving.

Easy Substitution: Make this recipe dairy-free by substituting dairy-free cheese for the mozzarella.

PER SERVING **CALORIES: 288; SATURATED FAT: 9G; TOTAL FAT: 23G; PROTEIN: 12G; TOTAL CARBS: 7G; FIBER: 1G; SODIUM: 595MG**

Cauliflower Salad with Cranberries and Almonds

SERVES
4 TO 6

PREP TIME:
15 MINUTES

MARINATE
TIME:
10 MINUTES

DAIRY-FREE

GF

GLUTEN-FREE

VEGETARIAN

30-MINUTE

The crunch of nuts paired with the subtle sweetness of cranberries and tart lemon in this healthy, cauliflower-based salad is downright heavenly. Speed up the prep by using a food processor to rice your cauliflower. You can store this salad in an airtight glass container in the refrigerator up to five days.

1 head cauliflower, finely chopped

1 garlic clove, minced

1 teaspoon dried oregano (optional)

Pinch salt, plus more to season

Dash freshly ground black pepper, plus more to season

3 tablespoons minced fresh cilantro

½ cup dried cranberries

½ cup almonds

Juice of 1 lemon

¼ cup extra-virgin olive oil

1. In a large bowl, combine the chopped cauliflower, garlic, dried oregano (if using), salt, black pepper, cilantro, cranberries, almonds (or nut or seed of choice), lemon juice, and olive oil.

2. Marinate for 10 minutes, allowing all the flavors to come together. Season to taste with salt and black pepper.

3. This dish can be served right away or refrigerated in an airtight container for later use.

Easy Substitution: Pumpkin seeds or walnuts can be used instead of almonds.

PER SERVING CALORIES: 317; SATURATED FAT: 3G; TOTAL FAT: 22G; PROTEIN: 7G; TOTAL CARBS: 29G; FIBER: 7G; SODIUM: 85MG

Chickpea Salad with Sliced Pita

This chickpea salad features onion, dill, basil, and lemon. It's good on its own or stuffed into a pita pocket. If you're not using it as a main dish, bring it to picnics and barbecues to serve as an appetizer.

SERVES
4 TO 6

PREP TIME:
20 MINUTES
PLUS 30
MINUTES TO
REST

DAIRY-FREE

VEGETARIAN

2 (15-ounce) cans chickpeas, drained and rinsed

3 tablespoons diced red onion

2 tablespoons minced fresh dill

2 tablespoons minced fresh cilantro

2 tablespoons minced fresh basil

½ cup black olives, halved

½ cup Kalamata olives, pitted

½ red pepper, seeded and diced

½ yellow pepper, seeded and diced

1 small cauliflower head, stemmed and diced

2 celery stalks, ends removed and diced

1 teaspoon dried oregano

Juice of 1 lemon

1 cup Italian vinaigrette

Pinch salt

Dash freshly ground black pepper

1 (15-ounce) package pita bread, sliced

1. In a large bowl, combine the chickpeas, onion, dill, cilantro, basil, black olives, Kalamata olives, red peppers, yellow peppers, cauliflower, celery, oregano, lemon juice, vinaigrette, salt, and black pepper, tossing to evenly coat.

2. Let the chickpea mixture rest at room temperature for 30 minutes so all the flavors can come together.

3. Serve with the pita bread.

Lunch Remix: This dish is a great next-day lunch at home or on the go—equally delicious over a bed of salad greens or with your favorite tortilla chips.

PER SERVING CALORIES: 572; SATURATED FAT: 3G; TOTAL FAT: 22G; PROTEIN: 15G; TOTAL CARBS: 82G; FIBER: 10G; SODIUM: 1613MG

Curried Tuna Salad

SERVES
4

PREP TIME:
10 MINUTES

DAIRY-FREE

GF

GLUTEN-FREE

30-MINUTE

After trying this recipe, you may never eat tuna any other way. The curry gives the fish a subtle, yet unexpected, kick, providing a delightful contrast to the natural sweetness of the apples. Fancy enough to bring to a party, this dish is also casual enough for a weeknight meal. Serve it over a simple salad or between two slices of your favorite sandwich bread, and dinner is ready.

2 (5-ounce) cans tuna, drained

½ onion, minced

1 celery stalk, ends removed and diced

½ cup mayonnaise

2 tablespoons yellow curry powder

½ apple, cored and diced

Pinch salt

Dash freshly ground black pepper

1. In a medium bowl, combine the tuna, onion, celery, mayonnaise, curry powder, apple, salt, and black pepper.

2. Serve immediately or store in an airtight glass container in your refrigerator up to five days.

Easy Substitution: For a slight variation, try substituting a ripe pear for the apple.

PER SERVING CALORIES: 276; SATURATED FAT: 3G; TOTAL FAT: 16G; PROTEIN: 20G; TOTAL CARBS: 14G; FIBER: 2G; SODIUM: 288MG

Cowboy "Caviar"

Cowboy "caviar" is a clever description for this inventive and healthy bean salad, jam-packed with tomatoes, red and green peppers, corn, fresh herbs, and avocado, and tossed in a zesty vinaigrette dressing. With its Tex-Mex flair, this dish is guaranteed to be a crowd-pleaser.

SERVES
4 TO 6

PREP TIME:
15 MINUTES

MARINATE TIME:
10 MINUTES

DAIRY-FREE

GF

GLUTEN-FREE

VEGETARIAN

(30)

30-MINUTE

FOR THE DRESSING

½ cup apple cider vinegar

½ cup extra-virgin olive oil

2 tablespoons real maple syrup

1 teaspoon dried oregano

1 teaspoon salt

Dash freshly ground black pepper

Juice of 1 lime

FOR THE SALAD

2 tomatoes, cored and diced

2 celery stalks, ends removed and diced

1 red pepper, seeded and diced

1 green pepper, seeded and diced

1 cup corn, fresh or frozen

3 tablespoons minced fresh cilantro

3 tablespoons minced scallions, white and green parts

½ red onion, minced

1 (15-ounce) can black-eyed peas, drained and rinsed

1 (15-ounce) can black beans, drained and rinsed

1 jalapeño pepper, seeded and diced (optional)

2 avocados, diced

continued

Cowboy "Caviar," continued

TO MAKE THE DRESSING

In a small bowl, fully combine the vinegar, oil, maple syrup, oregano, salt, black pepper, and lime juice.

TO MAKE THE SALAD

1. In a large bowl, toss the tomatoes, celery, red and green peppers, corn, cilantro, scallions, black-eyed peas, beans, jalapeño pepper, and avocado.

2. Pour the dressing over the salad and toss again.

3. Allow the salad to marinate for 5 to 10 minutes.

4. Serve immediately or store in an airtight container in the refrigerator up to five days.

Lunch Remix: Serve this dish the next day over a bed of greens, or with any type of corn or tortilla chips.

PER SERVING CALORIES: 591; SATURATED FAT: 6G; TOTAL FAT: 40G; PROTEIN: 13G; TOTAL CARBS: 53G; FIBER: 18G; SODIUM: 669MG

Smoked Turkey and Spinach Wraps

These wraps are nearly effortless to assemble. Feel free to add condiments like pickles, tomatoes, or my pesto (see page 33). To make this treat gluten-free, swap the flour wrap for a gluten-free version.

MAKES
4

PREP TIME:
10 MINUTES

DAIRY-FREE

30-MINUTE

4 (10-inch) flour tortilla wraps

4 tablespoons mayonnaise (equally divided among each wrap)

8 slices smoked turkey breast (equally divided among each wrap)

2 cups fresh spinach leaves (equally divided among each wrap)

1 cup fresh basil leaves (equally divided among each wrap)

1. Spread 1 tablespoon of mayonnaise on each sandwich wrap.

2. Layer two slices of turkey, ½ cup of spinach leaves, and ¼ cup of basil on each wrap.

3. Repeat step 2 for each of the remaining 3 wraps.

4. Roll the wraps like a burrito to serve.

5. If you're taking the wraps on the go, try placing each in parchment paper and halving them. (If you don't have parchment paper, halve the wraps, then cover them with aluminum foil.)

Troubleshooting: Never rolled a burrito? Once you have placed the ingredients in the center of your wrap, fold in the top and bottom of the wrap, then the sides, as snugly as you can, and roll up.

PER SERVING **CALORIES: 216; SATURATED FAT: 2G; TOTAL FAT: 9G; PROTEIN: 15G; TOTAL CARBS: 22G; FIBER: 1G; SODIUM: 987MG**

Roasted Pepper, Basil, and Mozzarella Sandwiches

MAKES
4

PREP TIME:
20 MINUTES

VEGETARIAN

30-MINUTE

This sandwich is essentially a caprese, with sweet, yet savory, roasted peppers instead of tomatoes. I make it all year, but it's particularly delightful in the summer, when fresh basil is in season.

4 bulky sandwich rolls

4 tablespoons mayonnaise (equally divided among each sandwich)

2 cups fresh basil leaves, stemmed (equally divided among each sandwich)

4 slices of roasted peppers (equally divided among each sandwich)

4 slices fresh mozzarella (equally divided among each sandwich)

Salt (equally divided among each sandwich)

Freshly ground black pepper (equally divided among each sandwich)

1. Spread 1 tablespoon of mayonnaise on each side of a sandwich roll.

2. Layer with 5 to 6 leaves of fresh basil, 1 slice of roasted pepper, and 1 slice of mozzarella.

3. Season with salt and black pepper, and top with the other half of the sandwich roll.

4. Repeat steps 2 and 3 for the remaining 3 rolls.

5. Serve immediately or place each roll in plastic wrap if you're taking them to go.

Easy Substitution: For a slight variation, try replacing the basil with spinach (and the roasted peppers with freshly sliced tomato).

PER SERVING CALORIES: 348; SATURATED FAT: 5G; TOTAL FAT: 12G; PROTEIN: 11G; TOTAL CARBS: 44G; FIBER: 2G; SODIUM: 606MG

Easy Vegetarian Taco Bowls

This recipe is easy Mexican food at its finest. The combination of beans, tomatoes, avocados, and other veggies works incredibly well with the simple vinaigrette dressing—a slightly acidic, slightly sweet combination of oil, vinegar, maple syrup, and lime juice.

SERVES
4 TO 6

PREP TIME:
20 MINUTES

GF
GLUTEN-FREE

VEGETARIAN

30-MINUTE

FOR THE DRESSING

½ cup extra-virgin olive oil

½ cup apple cider vinegar

2 tablespoons real maple syrup

Juice of 1 lime

1 teaspoon salt

Dash freshly ground black pepper

FOR THE BOWLS

1 head romaine lettuce, chopped

1 (15-ounce) can black beans, drained

2 tomatoes, cored and diced

2 cups corn, fresh or frozen

1 (6-ounce) can pitted black olives, drained and halved

2 avocados, diced

1 bunch fresh cilantro, minced

1 cup sharp Cheddar cheese (optional)

4 tablespoons sour cream (optional)

TO MAKE THE DRESSING

In a small bowl, whisk the oil, vinegar, maple syrup, lime juice, salt, and black pepper, until well combined.

continued

Easy Vegetarian Taco Bowls, continued

TO MAKE THE BOWLS

1. Place the romaine lettuce at the bottom of a large salad bowl.

2. Sprinkle the black beans over the lettuce.

3. Add the tomatoes, corn, black olives, avocado, and cilantro. Top with the Cheddar cheese (if using).

4. Pour the dressing over the whole salad, and toss well to coat.

5. Plate and serve with 1 tablespoon of sour cream (if using) for each.

6. Serve immediately or store in an airtight container up to two days in the refrigerator.

Troubleshooting: To remove an avocado pit, simply halve the avocado, stick a sharp knife into the pit, twist, and lift the pit out.

PER SERVING **CALORIES: 617; SATURATED FAT: 6G; TOTAL FAT: 45G; PROTEIN: 11G; TOTAL CARBS: 53G; FIBER: 16G; SODIUM: 877MG**

CHAPTER 3

5-Ingredient

Forget the page-long ingredient lists of cookbooks past. The recipes in this chapter take a decidedly "less is more" approach. You can make each of them with five or fewer ingredients (not counting oil, vinegar, salt, and black pepper).

‹ Lemon Chicken Piccata, page 39

Avocado Toast

DAIRY-FREE

VEGETARIAN

30-MINUTE

Avocado toast has become ubiquitous on fancy brunch menus across the country, and for good reason. This dish offers the perfect combination of lemony goodness with a salty flair and the buttery, melt-in-your-mouth finish that avocados always deliver. When made at home, this toast is relatively cheap, too—and it's not just for brunch!

4 slices bread, white or whole-grain

3 avocados, flesh scooped out (equally divided)

Juice of 1 lemon (equally divided)

4 pinches salt (equally divided)

4 dashes fresh ground black pepper (equally divided)

1 teaspoon chili flakes (equally divided, if using)

1. Toast the 4 slices of bread on medium heat in your toaster or toaster oven (or, if preferred, don't toast the bread).

2. Mash the avocado with a fork in a small bowl and spread evenly onto each of the four slices of toast.

3. Sprinkle each slice with equal parts of the lemon juice, 1 pinch of salt, 1 dash of black pepper, and ¼ teaspoon of chili flakes (if using), and serve immediately.

Troubleshooting: Selecting a ripe avocado is not always easy. Look for evenly dark avocados that are firm to the touch with a slight give. If the avocados are too ripe, the skins will be overly brown with dark blemishes, and when you apply pressure, will feel mushy.

PER SERVING **CALORIES: 330; SATURATED FAT: 3G; TOTAL FAT: 22G; PROTEIN: 7G; TOTAL CARBS: 32G; FIBER: 11G; SODIUM: 231MG**

Deviled Egg Salad

The secret weapon in this picnic favorite is the smoked paprika, which adds a dimension of flavor missing from a traditional deviled egg salad. I prefer to use this dish as an appetizer—or as a side for a party—but you can easily treat it like a main dish and supplement with a big salad. Alternatively, you could stuff the egg salad between two slices of bread for a delicious sandwich.

12 eggs, large

3 tablespoons mayonnaise

Pinch salt

Dash freshly ground black pepper

1 tablespoon smoked paprika

1. Submerge the eggs in a large pot three-quarters full of cold water over high heat and bring to boil.

2. Cook for 10 minutes, then remove from the heat and drain. Allow the eggs to cool for 5 minutes, then peel and slice.

3. In a medium bowl, mash the egg slices and combine with the mayonnaise, salt, black pepper, and smoked paprika.

4. Serve immediately, or store in an airtight container in the refrigerator up to five days.

Troubleshooting: Sometimes peeling eggs can be a challenge. After boiling the eggs, place them in a bowl of cold water for 5 minutes. Then peel the eggs under cool, running water. This method will make peeling eggs a snap!

PER SERVING **CALORIES: 237; SATURATED FAT: 5G; TOTAL FAT: 17G; PROTEIN: 17G; TOTAL CARBS: 5G; FIBER: 1G; SODIUM: 303MG**

SERVES
4 TO 6

PREP TIME:
10 MINUTES

COOK TIME:
15 MINUTES
PLUS
5 MINUTES
TO COOL

DAIRY-FREE

GF
GLUTEN-FREE

30-MINUTE

Mexican-Style Baked Eggs

SERVES
4 TO 5

PREP TIME:
5 MINUTES

COOK TIME:
30 MINUTES

DAIRY-FREE

GF

GLUTEN-FREE

VEGETARIAN

Making breakfast-y foods for dinner can be a fun change of pace. This recipe, in particular, takes minutes to assemble and, if my experience counts for anything, kids will love it. The combination of corn, black beans, olives, and eggs is the ideal Mexican-style comfort food. Feel free to top this dish with hot sauce, fresh cilantro, Cheddar cheese, sour cream, or a combination thereof. Try your favorite tortillas as a side.

1 (24-ounce) jar marinara

2 cups corn, fresh or frozen

1 (15-ounce) can black beans, drained and rinsed

1 cup black pitted olives, halved (optional)

6 eggs, large

Salt

Freshly ground black pepper

1. Preheat the oven to 400°F.

2. In a 9-by-13-inch oven-safe casserole dish, combine the marinara, corn, black beans, and olives.

3. Crack the eggs over the marinara mixture, and season with salt and black pepper.

4. Bake for 30 minutes or until the eggs are springy to the touch and the egg whites are set and firm. It's okay if the yolk centers are still a little runny.

5. Serve immediately.

Lunch Remix: This recipe can easily be doubled if you use a larger baking dish. Leftovers can be stored in an airtight container up to three days, portions of which can be reheated on the stove for quick breakfasts or lunches on the go.

PER SERVING **CALORIES: 380; SATURATED FAT: 3G; TOTAL FAT: 14G; PROTEIN: 19G; TOTAL CARBS: 47G; FIBER: 9G; SODIUM: 1451MG**

Fresh Summer Pesto Pasta

With a robust flavor and vibrant green color, pesto is a fantastically tasty (and incredibly Instagram-worthy) complement to a bowl of buoyant, al dente spaghetti. I generally double the pesto recipe, serving one batch for dinner and freezing the other. The pesto can stay in the freezer in an airtight container for one to two months.

SERVES
4 TO 6

PREP TIME:
5 MINUTES

COOK TIME:
15 MINUTES

FREEZER-
FRIENDLY

VEGETARIAN

30-MINUTE

FOR THE PESTO

4 cups fresh basil leaves

2 garlic cloves, minced

**1 cup grated Parmesan
(optional)**

½ cup raw pine nuts

1 teaspoon salt

Dash freshly ground black pepper

½ cup extra-virgin olive oil

FOR THE PASTA

Pinch salt

1 pound spaghetti pasta

TO MAKE THE PESTO

1. In a blender, blend on high speed the basil, garlic, Parmesan (if using), pine nuts, salt, and black pepper.

2. Set the blender speed on medium and gradually add the olive oil in a slow, steady stream.

3. Blend until smooth and all the ingredients are fully combined. Remove from the blender to a medium bowl and set aside.

TO MAKE THE PASTA

1. Add the pasta to a large pot of boiling water and cook according to the package instructions until al dente (still firm), about 10 to 12 minutes, and drain.

continued

Fresh Summer Pesto Pasta, continued

2. Immediately add 3 to 4 tablespoons of pesto and toss until the pasta is fully coated.

3. Serve immediately. If you're not freezing the pesto, you can store in an airtight container in the refrigerator up to three days.

Troubleshooting: If you don't have a blender, you can use a mortar and pestle, which is a small bowl and round mallet. Take the basil, garlic, pine nuts, salt, and black pepper, and mash into a paste. Then add the Parmesan and oil and grind with the pestle until the ingredients are fully combined. Making the pesto is that easy!

PER SERVING **CALORIES: 761; SATURATED FAT: 5G; TOTAL FAT: 39G; PROTEIN: 18G; TOTAL CARBS: 89G; FIBER: 5G; SODIUM: 590MG**

White Tortilla Pizzas

Crave pizza but don't have time to make one from scratch? Try a tortilla pizza. I personally love this simple white garlic version with broccoli and olive oil, but I would encourage you to try whatever toppings you like in subsequent iterations, like pepperoni, marinara, pesto, or other vegetables.

MAKES
4

PREP TIME:
10 MINUTES

COOK TIME:
10 MINUTES

VEGETARIAN

30-MINUTE

4 flour tortillas

4 tablespoons extra-virgin olive oil (divided among each tortilla)

2 garlic cloves, minced (divided among each tortilla)

1 cup finely chopped broccoli (divided among each tortilla)

1 red pepper, seeded and diced (divided among each tortilla)

4 pinches salt (divided among each tortilla)

4 dashes freshly ground black pepper (divided among each tortilla)

2½ cups shredded mozzarella (divided among each tortilla)

1. Preheat the oven to 425°F.

2. Spread the tortillas on a large sheet pan.

3. Drizzle each tortilla with 1 tablespoon of oil. Then, sprinkle each with ¼ of the garlic, ¼ cup of the broccoli, ¼ of the red pepper, 1 pinch of salt, 1 dash of black pepper, and ¼ of the shredded mozzarella.

4. Bake for 10 minutes, until the tortillas are golden brown.

5. Serve and enjoy.

Pair With: These pizzas would be fabulous with the Tomato and Caper Pasta Salad (see page 99).

PER SERVING **CALORIES: 480; SATURATED FAT: 12G; TOTAL FAT: 30G; PROTEIN: 23G; TOTAL CARBS: 33G; FIBER: 3G; SODIUM: 1014MG**

Flatbread Chicken Salad Sandwiches

MAKES
4

PREP TIME:
15 MINUTES

DAIRY-FREE

30-MINUTE

These chicken salad sandwiches are a great way to use up leftovers from a roasted whole chicken, although you could also purchase pre-cooked chicken if you're in a pinch. The fresh pomegranate seeds and lemon make this chicken salad special. For the bread, I prefer the soft, pliability of flatbread, which I find perfect for sandwiches.

4 cups pre-cooked chicken, shredded

1 cup pomegranate seeds

½ cup mayonnaise

Juice of 1 lemon

Pinch salt

Dash freshly ground black pepper

4 flatbreads

1. In a medium bowl, combine the chicken, pomegranate seeds, mayonnaise, lemon juice, salt, and black pepper.

2. To assemble the sandwiches, place 1 cup of the chicken salad on each piece of flatbread. Fold in the lower and upper sides first, then roll up like a burrito.

3. Serve immediately or wrap each sandwich individually in plastic wrap and store in an airtight container in the refrigerator up to four days.

Lunch Remix: Serve the chicken salad throughout the week over a bed of salad greens, or as a starter with tortilla chips.

PER SERVING CALORIES: 466; SATURATED FAT: 3G; TOTAL FAT: 20G; PROTEIN: 39G; TOTAL CARBS: 27G; FIBER: 2G; SODIUM: 565MG

Easy BLTs

There's a reason people keep returning to the BLT: It's a classic. And in terms of how much flavor this sandwich packs into just a few ingredients, the BLT really can't be beat. There's something undeniable about the appeal of salty bacon paired with a generous spread of mayonnaise, juicy tomatoes, and crisp lettuce. Naturally, this recipe will taste better in the summer when tomatoes are at their peak, but any time is the right time for a BLT.

MAKES
4

PREP TIME:
5 MINUTES

COOK TIME:
20 MINUTES

DAIRY-FREE

30-MINUTE

16 bacon slices (divided among each sandwich)

8 slices bread, white or whole-grain

4 tablespoons mayonnaise (divided among each sandwich)

8 tomato slices (divided among each sandwich)

8 romaine lettuce leaves (divided among each sandwich)

1. Preheat the oven to 400°F.

2. Line a large sheet pan with parchment paper (or aluminum foil), and place the bacon in a single layer.

3. Bake for 20 minutes, or until the bacon reaches your desired crispiness.

4. To assemble the sandwiches, spread ½ tablespoon of the mayonnaise across each bread slice, and layer each sandwich with 2 tomato slices, 2 pieces of romaine lettuce, and 4 bacon slices.

5. Serve and enjoy.

Easy Substitution: Get creative and give these a gourmet flair by adding some fresh basil or a smear of pesto (see page 33), or both.

PER SERVING **CALORIES: 616; SATURATED FAT: 12G; TOTAL FAT: 39G; PROTEIN: 36G; TOTAL CARBS: 30G; FIBER: 4G; SODIUM: 2128MG**

White Wine and Garlic Shrimp Skillet

SERVES
4

PREP TIME:
10 MINUTES

COOK TIME:
10 MINUTES

DAIRY-FREE

GF

GLUTEN-FREE

30-MINUTE

Few things go together as well as white wine and garlic. And few proteins exhibit the subtle, yet fragrant, combination of flavors more effectively than shrimp. All this simple weeknight meal requires is one large skillet, a few choice ingredients, and voilà! You've got a fancy dinner on your table with next-to-no cleanup.

2 tablespoons extra-virgin olive oil

4 garlic cloves, minced

2 pounds shrimp, deveined and peeled

Pinch salt

Dash freshly ground black pepper

2 tablespoons minced fresh parsley

Juice of ½ lemon

1 cup white wine

1. In a large skillet, heat the oil over medium heat until hot.

2. Add the garlic and sauté for 1 to 2 minutes to infuse the oil.

3. Add the shrimp, salt, black pepper, and parsley, and sauté for 2 minutes or until the shrimp begins to turn pink. Add the lemon juice and white wine, and cook another 5 minutes, until the shrimp is pink and just cooked.

4. Serve immediately.

Pair With: The Cilantro Lime Rice (see page 101) and Simple Sweet Potato Fries (see page 104) complement this dish especially well.

PER SERVING CALORIES: 317; SATURATED FAT: 1G; TOTAL FAT: 9G; PROTEIN: 46G; TOTAL CARBS: 3G; FIBER: 0G; SODIUM: 306MG

Lemon Chicken Piccata

You've likely seen (or ordered) this dish on the menu at your favorite Italian restaurant. Well, turns out, this one is super easy to make at home. Nothing beats the savory, citrusy mélange of lemon, white wine, chicken, and herbs. And since you can make this recipe all in one pan, cleanup is a breeze.

SERVES
4

PREP TIME:
10 MINUTES

COOK TIME:
25 MINUTES

GF

GLUTEN-FREE

1 tablespoon extra-virgin olive oil

1 tablespoon unsalted butter

1 pound boneless, skinless chicken breast, thinly sliced

3 tablespoons minced fresh parsley

Pinch salt

Dash freshly ground black pepper

½ cup white wine

Juice of 1 lemon

1. In a large skillet, heat the oil and butter over medium heat until the butter has melted.

2. Add the chicken, parsley, salt, and black pepper, and sauté for 5 minutes, until the chicken begins to firm.

3. Reduce to medium-low heat, and add the white wine and lemon juice. Simmer for 15 minutes, so all the flavors can come together and the chicken cooks through.

4. Serve immediately.

Pair With: The Garlic Mashed Potatoes (see page 103) would go particularly well with this recipe, or serve it with the salad or pasta of your choice.

PER SERVING CALORIES: 213; SATURATED FAT: 2G; TOTAL FAT: 9G; PROTEIN: 24G; TOTAL CARBS: 1 G; FIBER: 0G; SODIUM: 122MG

Marinated Asian-Style Chicken

SERVES
4 TO 6

PREP TIME:
5 MINUTES

MARINATE
TIME:
30 MINUTES

COOK TIME:
30 MINUTES

DAIRY-FREE

The combination of honey, soy sauce, and barbecue sauce gives this chicken the salty-sweet flavor you crave—especially during grilling season. This recipe is designed for the grill to give the chicken some extra char. But if you don't have a grill, you can always spread these out on a sheet pan (after step 2), and bake them for 30 minutes at 400°F (or until the chicken reaches an internal temperature of 165°F).

8 chicken thighs or drumsticks

¾ cup barbecue sauce

½ cup soy sauce

3 tablespoons honey

Pinch salt

Dash freshly ground black pepper

2 garlic cloves, sliced

1. In a large bowl, combine the barbecue sauce, soy sauce, honey, salt, black pepper, and garlic. Add the chicken and toss until well coated.

2. Marinate for at least 30 minutes in the refrigerator.

3. Preheat your grill to medium-high heat.

4. Grill the chicken and cook for about 15 minutes on each side, until crispy and fully cooked, or until the internal temperature reaches 165°F.

5. Serve and enjoy.

Pair With: Try the Mediterranean Potato Salad (see page 100) or Lemon Quinoa Salad (see page 98).

PER SERVING CALORIES: 401; SATURATED FAT: 5G; TOTAL FAT: 18G; PROTEIN: 28G; TOTAL CARBS: 33G; FIBER: 1G; SODIUM: 2474MG

CHAPTER 4

One-Pot & Skillet

Don't let the thought of cleaning a pile of pots, pans, and plates ruin your enjoyment of the meal you've just made. All of the recipes in this chapter can be prepared with a single pot or pan (and the occasional mixing bowl). The result? Delicious, easy-to-make stir-fries, stews, and curries—with minimal post-dinner cleanup.

‹ Turkey Burgers with Caramelized Onions, page 55

Butter Bean Stew

SERVES
2 TO 4

PREP TIME:
20 MINUTES

COOK TIME:
25 MINUTES

DAIRY-FREE

FREEZER-
FRIENDLY

GF

GLUTEN-FREE

VEGETARIAN

This butter bean stew is a soulful, nourishing dish for cold days when all you want to do is stay huddled up inside. Full of nutritious veggies, this stew is packed with flavors both sweet and spicy, and tastes great over a steaming bed of white rice. Don't be afraid to make some extra and freeze the rest—it'll stay good up to three months in the freezer.

2 tablespoons extra-virgin olive oil

2 tablespoons peeled and minced fresh ginger

3 garlic cloves, minced

3 tablespoons minced fresh cilantro

2 tablespoons minced fresh basil

3 cups fresh spinach leaves

½ red pepper, seeded and sliced

½ yellow pepper, seeded and sliced

½ teaspoon cinnamon

2 pinches salt, divided

2 dashes freshly ground black pepper, divided

½ teaspoon yellow curry powder, plus 1 tablespoon (½ teaspoon used first, then 1 tablespoon used later)

2 (15-ounce) cans butter beans, drained and rinsed

1 (13.5-ounce) can full-fat coconut milk

2 tablespoons real maple syrup

1. In a medium pot, heat the oil over medium heat.

2. Add the ginger, garlic, cilantro, and basil, and sauté for 2 to 3 minutes to infuse the oil.

3. Add the spinach, red peppers, yellow peppers, cinnamon, a pinch of salt, a dash of black pepper, and ½ teaspoon curry powder, and sauté another 5 minutes, until the spinach begins to wilt.

4. Add the beans, coconut milk, maple syrup, 1 tablespoon of curry powder, a pinch of salt, and a dash of black pepper. Bring to a boil, then immediately reduce to low heat and simmer for 15 minutes.

5. Serve immediately or let cool and store refrigerated in an airtight container up to three days.

Pair With: The Cilantro Lime Rice (see page 101) would be a lovely addition to this stew.

PER SERVING **CALORIES: 459; SATURATED FAT: 18G; TOTAL FAT: 27G; PROTEIN: 14G; TOTAL CARBS: 45G; FIBER: 12G; SODIUM: 114MG**

Easy Mexican-Style Pinto Beans

SERVES
4 TO 6

PREP TIME:
10 MINUTES

COOK TIME:
25 MINUTES

DAIRY-FREE

FREEZER-
FRIENDLY

GF

GLUTEN-FREE

VEGETARIAN

This fresh Mexican stew, spiked with chili powder and ground cumin, is ideal for both backyard barbecues and cozy nights-in alike. You can keep this recipe simple or spice things up with a variety of toppings, like hot sauce, sliced jalapeños, and Cheddar cheese. Eat this dish on its own, or, if you've got some tortillas on hand, use as a filling for tacos or burritos. Leftovers can be frozen in a freezer-friendly container up to three months.

2 tablespoons extra-virgin olive oil

1 onion, minced

Pinch salt

Dash freshly ground black pepper

2 garlic cloves, minced

2 tablespoons fresh minced cilantro

4 (15-ounce) cans pinto beans, rinsed, drained, and divided

1 (15-ounce) can pinto beans, puréed in a high-speed blender, drained

1½ tablespoons chili powder

1½ tablespoons ground cumin

¼ cup apple cider vinegar

2 tablespoons real maple syrup

1 cup low-sodium vegetable stock

1. In a medium pot, heat the oil over medium heat for 2 minutes, or until hot.

2. Add the onion, salt, and black pepper, and sauté for 2 minutes to infuse the oil.

3. Add the garlic and cilantro, and sauté for 1 minute.

4. Add the pinto beans, both whole and puréed, plus the chili powder, cumin, vinegar, maple syrup, and stock.

5. Bring to a quick boil, then reduce to low heat and simmer for 15 minutes.

6. Serve immediately or let cool and store refrigerated in an airtight container up to three days.

Troubleshooting: To purée pinto beans, add the drained beans to your blender. Purée on high for 2 to 3 minutes, until the beans have reached a smooth consistency.

PER SERVING CALORIES: 581; SATURATED FAT: 2G; TOTAL FAT: 10G; PROTEIN: 30G; TOTAL CARBS: 97G; FIBER: 31G; SODIUM: 268MG

Skillet Beef Tacos

SERVES
4

PREP TIME:
10 MINUTES

COOK TIME:
30 MINUTES

DAIRY-FREE

FREEZER-
FRIENDLY

GF
GLUTEN-FREE

This is one of my go-to recipes on busy days—a budget-friendly dinner with just the right amount of spice. This dish is on the simpler side, so I'd encourage you to add your own fixings, like sliced black olives, sour cream, and Cheddar cheese. You can store leftovers in an airtight container in the freezer up to three months.

2 tablespoons extra-virgin olive oil

1 small onion, minced

2 garlic cloves, minced

3 tablespoons minced fresh cilantro

1 pound ground beef

1½ tablespoons ground cumin

1 tablespoon chili powder

1 (15-ounce) can kidney beans or black beans, drained and rinsed

1½ cups low-sodium chicken stock or water

1 cup mild salsa

Tortillas or corn taco shells (optional)

1. In a large skillet, heat the oil over medium heat for 2 minutes, or until hot.

2. Add the onion, garlic, and cilantro, and sauté for 2 minutes.

3. Add the beef and continue to cook for another 5 minutes, or until the beef begins to brown.

4. Add the cumin, chili powder, beans, stock, and salsa. Bring to a quick boil for 2 minutes, then reduce to low heat and simmer for 15 minutes.

5. Serve immediately on tortillas (if using) or let cool and refrigerate in an airtight container up to four days.

Pair With: My Easy Guacamole (see page 96), of course.

PER SERVING CALORIES: 478; SATURATED FAT: 8G; TOTAL FAT: 27G; PROTEIN: 37G; TOTAL CARBS: 22G; FIBER: 6G; SODIUM: 539MG

Asian Veggie Stir-Fry

If you're looking for a stress-free weeknight dinner, look no further. I prefer to make this veggie stir-fry with broccoli, onion, and ginger, but other vegetables, like sugar snap peas, red peppers, or kale, will work just as well. In any event, my easy sweet-and-salty sauce, made with honey, soy sauce, and Chinese five-spice powder, will provide an incredible depth of flavor.

SERVES
4 TO 6

PREP TIME:
15 MINUTES

COOK TIME:
20 MINUTES

DAIRY-FREE

GF

GLUTEN-FREE

VEGETARIAN

FOR THE SAUCE

1 cup soy sauce

1 tablespoon honey

1 teaspoon Chinese five-spice powder

1 tablespoon corn starch

FOR THE STIR-FRY

1 tablespoon coconut oil

1 tablespoon peeled and minced fresh ginger

2 tablespoons minced fresh cilantro

2 garlic cloves, minced

1 large onion, sliced

Pinch salt

Dash freshly ground black pepper

4 large broccoli florets, chopped

TO MAKE THE SAUCE

In a medium bowl, whisk the soy sauce, honey, Chinese five-spice and corn starch until well combined.

TO MAKE THE STIR-FRY

1. In a large wok or large skillet, heat the coconut oil over high heat until hot. Add the ginger, cilantro, and garlic, and sauté for 1 minute.

continued

one-pot & skillet 49

Asian Veggie Stir-Fry, continued

2. Add the onion, salt, black pepper, and broccoli and sauté for 5 minutes, or until the onions become translucent.

3. Add the sauce and simmer on low heat for 10 minutes, or until the broccoli is tender.

4. Serve immediately.

Lunch Remix: Try reheating this dish the next day for brunch or lunch with a fried egg on top.

PER SERVING **CALORIES: 141; SATURATED FAT: 3G; TOTAL FAT: 4G; PROTEIN: 7G; TOTAL CARBS: 23G; FIBER: 4G; SODIUM: 3665MG**

Shrimp and Sausage Sauté

This is my go-to meal for a chilly evening—and is easy to adjust to dietary restrictions or preferences. If you want to ditch the meat, add more shrimp; if you want to ditch the seafood, add more sausage (or the vegetable of your choice). And for a true indulgence, sprinkle some Cheddar cheese on top before serving.

SERVES
4 TO 6

PREP TIME:
10 MINUTES

COOK TIME:
35 MINUTES

DAIRY-FREE

GF

GLUTEN-FREE

2 tablespoons extra-virgin olive oil

1 onion, minced

4 garlic cloves, minced

4 celery stalks, ends removed and chopped

Pinch salt

Dash freshly ground black pepper

1 tablespoon dried oregano

3 tablespoons minced fresh parsley

3 sausage links, removed from casings and crumbled

1 (28-ounce) jar marinara

2 cups white or basmati rice

1 pound shrimp, deveined and peeled

1. In a medium pot, heat the oil over medium heat.

2. Add the onion, garlic, celery, salt, black pepper, oregano, and parsley, and sauté for 5 minutes.

3. Add the sausage and sauté for another 8 minutes. Then add the marinara sauce and bring the mixture to a boil.

4. Add the rice, reduce to medium-low heat, and cover.

continued

Shrimp and Sausage Sauté, continued

5. Cook for 15 minutes, or until the rice begins to be tender. Then add the shrimp and cook for another 5 minutes until the shrimp is just cooked (firm and pink in color).

6. Serve immediately. Leftovers can be refrigerated in an airtight container up to three days.

Lunch Remix: Try reheating this one the next day and topping with a fried egg.

PER SERVING CALORIES: 728; SATURATED FAT: 6G; TOTAL FAT: 24G; PROTEIN: 39G; TOTAL CARBS: 92G; FIBER: 6G; SODIUM: 1239MG

Garlic Shrimp Risotto

This creamy, garlicky risotto paired with juicy shrimp and sweet peas is guaranteed to leave you satisfied. Risotto can seem intimidating, but it's essentially just a type of rice. Use this recipe to surprise your family and friends with a mid-week gourmet dinner. You won't regret spending the time and effort!

SERVES
4 TO 6

PREP TIME:
10 MINUTES

COOK TIME:
25 MINUTES

GF
GLUTEN-FREE

1 tablespoon extra-virgin olive oil

1 tablespoon unsalted butter

1 small shallot, minced

5 garlic cloves, minced

Pinch salt

Dash freshly ground black pepper, plus more for garnish

1 teaspoon dried oregano

2 tablespoons minced fresh parsley

1 thyme sprig (optional)

2 cups risotto

4 cups low-sodium chicken or vegetable stock (adding ½ cup at a time)

1 (8-ounce) container heavy cream

1 cup fresh or frozen peas

1 pound shrimp, deveined and peeled

Parmesan cheese, for garnish

1. In a large skillet, heat the oil and butter over medium heat.

2. Add the shallots, garlic, salt, black pepper, oregano, parsley, and thyme (if using) and sauté for 4 to 5 minutes, or until the shallots become translucent.

3. Add the risotto and sauté for another 2 minutes.

4. Add the stock ½ cup at a time, in one-minute intervals, while continuing to stir. The risotto will slowly absorb the stock. Once all the stock is added, cook for 10 to 15 minutes, or until the risotto is firm but tender.

continued

Garlic Shrimp Risotto, continued

5. Add the cream along with the peas and shrimp. Reduce to low heat and simmer for 5 minutes, or until the peas and shrimp become tender.

6. Toss gently and garnish with freshly ground black pepper and Parmesan.

7. Serve immediately or let cool and store in an airtight container in the refrigerator up to two days.

Troubleshooting: A common mistake people make with risotto is not cooking it long enough. Make sure to stick to the directions, and cook until firm but tender. Feel free to try a bite while it's still cooking if you're uncertain, just be sure not to burn your tongue!

PER SERVING **CALORIES: 781; SATURATED FAT: 16G; TOTAL FAT: 31G; PROTEIN: 35G; TOTAL CARBS: 91G; FIBER: 5G; SODIUM: 329MG**

Turkey Burgers with Caramelized Onions

Introducing your new favorite turkey burger recipe. The sweet caramelized onions, in particular, pack a ton of flavor, but make sure you pile these high with all the recipe's fixings. I promise they'll taste just as good, if not better, than any beef burger you're likely to cook at home. If you want to store a few for later, make extra and double-wrap them in a freezer-friendly bag.

MAKES
4

PREP TIME:
10 MINUTES

COOK TIME:
30 MINUTES

DAIRY-FREE

FREEZER-FRIENDLY

1 pound ground turkey

2 pinches salt, divided

2 dashes freshly ground black pepper, divided

1 tablespoon Worcestershire sauce

1½ tablespoons ketchup

2 tablespoons extra-virgin olive oil

1 large onion, sliced

8 mushrooms, stemmed and sliced

½ cup water

4 hamburger buns

1. In a medium bowl, mix by hand the ground turkey, a pinch of salt, a dash of black pepper, Worcestershire sauce, and ketchup. Form the mixture into four patties and set aside.

2. In a large skillet, heat the oil over medium heat.

3. Add the onions, mushrooms, and a pinch of salt and a dash of black pepper, and sauté for 8 minutes, or until the onions become translucent.

4. Move the onion and mushrooms to one side of the skillet and add the patties. Cook the patties for about 8 minutes on each side, or until they've reached an internal temperature of 160°F.

continued

Turkey Burgers with Caramelized Onions, continued

5. Add the water to the skillet and bring to a quick boil, then imme-
    diately reduce to low heat and let simmer for 10 minutes.

6. Serve immediately on hamburger buns. Leftovers can be refrig-
    erated in an airtight container up to three days.

Pair With: The Mediterranean Potato Salad (see page 100) or Simple Sweet
Potato Fries (see page 104) are perfect sides to pair with this recipe.

PER SERVING **CALORIES: 381; SATURATED FAT: 4G; TOTAL FAT: 18G; PROTEIN: 26G; TOTAL
CARBS: 28G; FIBER: 2G; SODIUM: 498MG**

Turkey Sloppy Joes

We all grew up with a variation of the sloppy joe. We're familiar with the flavors—the slightly tangy mix of tomato sauce and beans—and we're familiar with the mess, which is kind of the point. For a more well-rounded dinner, pair this recipe with a quick green salad or roasted vegetables. Don't forget the napkins!

MAKES
4

PREP TIME:
10 MINUTES

COOK TIME:
25 MINUTES

DAIRY-FREE

2 tablespoons extra-virgin olive oil

1 onion, minced

2 garlic cloves, minced

1 pound ground turkey

Pinch salt

Dash freshly ground black pepper

1 (28-ounce) jar marinara

1 (16-ounce) can kidney beans, drained

2 tablespoons ketchup

1 tablespoon yellow mustard

4 bulky rolls

1. In a large skillet, heat the oil over medium heat.

2. Add the onion and garlic and sauté for 2 minutes to infuse the oil.

3. Add the ground turkey, salt, and black pepper, and sauté for another 5 minutes.

4. Add the marinara, kidney beans, ketchup, and mustard, and bring to a boil, then immediately reduce to low heat. Simmer for 15 minutes to ensure the meat is cooked through.

5. Spoon the meat evenly onto bulky rolls, and serve.

Lunch Remix: Revamp this dish the next day by spooning it over your favorite pasta.

PER SERVING **CALORIES: 420; SATURATED FAT: 4G; TOTAL FAT: 19G; PROTEIN: 27G; TOTAL CARBS: 37G; FIBER: 5G; SODIUM: 1521MG**

Easy Chicken Cacciatore

SERVES
2 TO 4

PREP TIME:
10 MINUTES

COOK TIME:
45 MINUTES

DAIRY-FREE

GF

GLUTEN-FREE

This Italian classic is a robustly flavorful, rustic dish. If you're short on time (or ingredients), you can pair this recipe with some simple white rice or roasted veggies for a more well-rounded meal.

2 tablespoons extra-virgin olive oil

1 yellow onion, diced

1 red onion, diced

4 garlic cloves, minced

1 tablespoon dried oregano

1 tablespoon dried thyme

1 teaspoon salt

Dash freshly ground black pepper

1 pound boneless, skinless chicken, sliced

1 red pepper, sliced and diced

1 yellow pepper, sliced and diced

1 green pepper, sliced and diced

1 (32-ounce) jar marinara

1. In a large skillet, heat the oil over medium heat.

2. Add the yellow onions, red onions, garlic, oregano, thyme, salt, and black pepper and sauté for 8 to 10 minutes, or until the onions are translucent and caramelized to a golden brown color.

3. Add the sliced chicken and sauté for 5 minutes.

4. Add the red, yellow, and green peppers and cook for another 5 minutes, or until the peppers are softened.

5. Add the marinara sauce and bring to a boil, then reduce to low heat and simmer for 20 minutes.

6. Serve immediately, or let cool and refrigerate in an airtight container up to four days.

Lunch Remix: This dish is one that's almost better the next day. Fancy it up with a dash of hot sauce or a sprinkle of Cheddar cheese.

PER SERVING **CALORIES: 294; SATURATED FAT: 1G; TOTAL FAT: 9G; PROTEIN: 31G; TOTAL CARBS: 26G; FIBER: 7G; SODIUM: 1841MG**

Chicken Red Curry

Normally, you'd have to order this dish for delivery from your favorite Thai spot. But now you can make this classic at home! The sweetness of the coconut milk mixed with the subtle spice of red curry creates an inimitable mix of flavors. Pair with white rice and toss the leftovers over thin egg noodles (think: lo mein) for two great, easy meals.

SERVES
2 TO 4

PREP TIME:
10 MINUTES

COOK TIME:
45 MINUTES

DAIRY-FREE

GF

GLUTEN-FREE

1 tablespoon extra-virgin olive oil

1 garlic clove, minced

1 tablespoon peeled and minced fresh ginger

1 small onion, minced

Pinch salt

Dash freshly ground black pepper

1 pound boneless skinless chicken, cut into cubes

1 tablespoon minced fresh cilantro

3 tablespoons red curry paste

1 (13.5-ounce) can full-fat coconut milk

3 tablespoons real maple syrup

1 tablespoon fish sauce

1. In a medium pot, heat the oil over medium heat.

2. Add the garlic, ginger, onion, salt, and black pepper, and sauté for 5 minutes.

3. Add the chicken and cilantro and sauté for an additional 5 minutes or until the chicken starts to become firm. Then add the red curry paste, coconut milk, maple syrup, and fish sauce.

4. Bring to a boil, then immediately reduce the heat to low and cook for another 20 minutes.

5. Serve immediately or let cool and refrigerate in an airtight container up to three days.

Easy Substitution: Make this recipe vegetarian by switching out the chicken for a pound of tofu or broccoli.

PER SERVING CALORIES: 466; SATURATED FAT: 22G; TOTAL FAT: 31G; PROTEIN: 29G; TOTAL CARBS: 21G; FIBER: 3G; SODIUM: 1063MG

CHAPTER 5

Sheet Pan & Baking Dish

Spread your well-seasoned ingredients on a sheet pan, place the pan in the oven, and, voilà, dinner is served. That's the beauty of the sheet pan recipes in this chapter, which also includes a few satisfying meals prepared in a baking dish. Easy peasy!

‹ Miso Sheet Pan Salmon, page 63

Sheet Pan Veggie Quesadillas

MAKES
4

PREP TIME:
10 MINUTES

COOK TIME:
20 MINUTES

VEGETARIAN

30-MINUTE

These easy sheet pan quesadillas—baked, not fried—are great for entertaining or on busy nights when you need dinner on the table fast. Even the pickiest of eaters can't resist the gooey, melted cheese and crisp tortilla. Keep the dish simple or pile it high with all the fixings: hot sauce, salsa, sour cream, sliced jalapeño, olives, fresh cilantro, and Easy Guacamole (see page 96).

8 flour tortillas

12 tablespoons refried beans (divided among each tortilla)

8 slices Cheddar cheese (divided among each tortilla)

2 cups fresh spinach leaves (divided among each tortilla)

1. Preheat the oven to 350°F. Line a large sheet pan with parchment paper (or aluminum foil).

2. Place a tortilla on the lined sheet pan. Add 3 tablespoons of refried beans, 2 slices of Cheddar cheese, and ½ cup spinach. Lay another tortilla on top, like a sandwich.

3. Repeat step 2 three more times to prepare the other quesadillas.

4. Bake all quesadillas for 20 minutes, or until crispy and golden brown.

5. Remove from the oven, slice each quesadilla in quarters, and serve immediately.

Easy Substitution: If you're looking for a fun variation, substitute broccoli and red pepper (or pre-cooked chicken) for the spinach.

PER SERVING **CALORIES: 461; SATURATED FAT: 13G; TOTAL FAT: 24G; PROTEIN: 22G; TOTAL CARBS: 40G; FIBER: 5G; SODIUM: 885MG**

Miso Sheet Pan Salmon

No Japanese takeout necessary! The sweetness of honey paired with the unique flavor of miso makes this one of my favorites. And if you're looking for a simple next-day lunch, leftovers will taste fantastic over a bed of greens.

SERVES
4

PREP TIME:
10 MINUTES

COOK TIME:
20 MINUTES

DAIRY-FREE

30-MINUTE

FOR THE SAUCE

½ cup soy sauce

3 tablespoons honey

2 tablespoons miso paste

FOR THE FISH

4 (1-inch thick) salmon fillets

1 large white onion, sliced

1 teaspoon salt

Dash freshly ground black pepper

3 tablespoons extra-virgin olive oil

TO MAKE THE SAUCE

Combine the soy sauce, honey, and miso paste in a small bowl and set aside.

TO MAKE THE FISH

1. Preheat the oven to 425°F and line a large sheet pan with parchment paper (or aluminum foil).

2. Lay the salmon on the sheet pan, then place the onions evenly around the fish.

3. Season the fish with salt and black pepper, then drizzle each fillet evenly with sauce and the oil. Bake for 20 minutes.

4. Serve immediately. Leftovers can be refrigerated in an airtight container up to three days.

Troubleshooting: Salmon can easily be overcooked, so bake for 15 minutes for medium-rare, and 20 minutes for well-done.

PER SERVING **CALORIES: 409; SATURATED FAT: 5G; TOTAL FAT: 27G; PROTEIN: 22G; TOTAL CARBS: 23G; FIBER: 2G; SODIUM: 2751MG**

White Fish with Roasted Tomatoes and Garlic

SERVES
4

PREP TIME:
5 MINUTES

COOK TIME:
20 MINUTES

DAIRY-FREE

GF

GLUTEN-FREE

30-MINUTE

If you're looking for a dish to give you that gourmet, fancy feel during the busy workweek, look no further. White wine and garlic infuse the fish and roasted tomatoes with intense, yet delicate, flavor. This recipe will go great with one or any number of sides from chapter 7, like the Mediterranean Potato Salad (see page 100), Tomato and Caper Pasta Salad (see page 99), Garlic Mashed Potatoes (see page 103), Cilantro Lime Rice (see page 101), Lemon Quinoa Salad (see page 98), or Simple Sweet Potato Fries (see page 104).

2 pounds white fish (haddock or flounder)

1 cup white wine

½ cup extra-virgin olive oil

1 pint cherry tomatoes

5 garlic cloves, minced

Salt

Freshly ground black pepper

1. Preheat the oven to 450°F.

2. Place the fish in an oven-safe baking dish and pour the white wine on the fish. Add the oil.

3. Place the tomatoes and garlic around the fish, and season the whole dish with salt and black pepper.

4. Bake for 20 minutes.

5. Serve immediately. Leftovers can be refrigerated in an airtight container up to two days.

Troubleshooting: A common mistake with light white fish is overcooking. If you like your fish more well done, add 5 minutes to the bake time for a total of 25 minutes. Any more and you'll overcook the fish.

PER SERVING CALORIES: 450; SATURATED FAT: 4G; TOTAL FAT: 27G; PROTEIN: 37G; TOTAL CARBS: 6G; FIBER: 1G; SODIUM: 762MG

Sheet Pan Barbecue Chicken and Roasted Veggies

Tangy, rich, crispy chicken and roasted onions and broccoli—what more could you ask for? Serve this dish on a night you're short on time, but still want to make a really special meal to bring everyone together. I love Woodstock Foods Original BBQ Sauce, although you can use whichever barbecue sauce you like.

SERVES
4 TO 6

PREP TIME:
10 MINUTES

COOK TIME:
25 MINUTES

DAIRY-FREE

GF

GLUTEN-FREE

8 boneless, skinless chicken thighs

½ cup barbecue sauce

1 large red onion, sliced

2 zucchinis, ends removed and cut

2 or 3 small heads broccoli, ends removed and cut

Salt

Freshly ground black pepper

3 tablespoons extra-virgin olive oil

1. Preheat the oven to 425°F.

2. Line a large, rimmed sheet pan with parchment paper (or aluminum foil).

3. Lay the chicken on the sheet pan, and pour the barbecue sauce evenly over each piece.

4. Place the onions, zucchini, and broccoli around the chicken, then season with salt and black pepper, and drizzle the oil over the entire pan.

continued

Sheet Pan Barbecue Chicken and Roasted Veggies, continued

5. Bake for 25 minutes, until the chicken is cooked through and the veggies are roasted.

6. Serve immediately. Leftovers can be refrigerated in an airtight container up to four days.

Pair With: This recipe will go great with my Mediterranean Potato Salad (see page 100) or Tomato and Caper Pasta Salad (see page 99). Or both!

PER SERVING **CALORIES: 422; SATURATED FAT: 2G; TOTAL FAT: 23G; PROTEIN: 36G; TOTAL CARBS: 27G; FIBER: 6G; SODIUM: 445MG**

Honey Mustard Glazed Sheet Pan Chicken

The sweetness of honey and the tang of Dijon make for a wonderfully balanced pairing of flavors. Serve this dish with the Mediterranean Potato Salad (see page 100), Garlic Mashed Potatoes (see page 103), or Simple Sweet Potato Fries (see page 104), and reheat leftovers the next day for a stress-free lunch or dinner.

SERVES
4

PREP TIME:
10 MINUTES

COOK TIME:
25 MINUTES

DAIRY-FREE

GF

GLUTEN-FREE

2 pounds boneless, skinless chicken thighs

Salt

Freshly ground black pepper

3 tablespoons Dijon mustard

2 tablespoons honey

2 tablespoons minced fresh parsley

1. Preheat the oven to 400°F.

2. Line a large, rimmed sheet pan with parchment paper (or aluminum foil).

3. Place the chicken thighs on the sheet pan, and season with salt and black pepper.

4. Use a spatula to coat each chicken thigh with Dijon mustard. Then coat each thigh with the honey.

5. Sprinkle the fresh parsley over the pan.

6. Bake for 25 minutes, or until the internal temperature of the chicken breasts is 165°F.

7. Serve immediately. Leftovers can be refrigerated in an airtight container up to four days.

Easy Substitution: Bone-in chicken thighs, boneless, skinless chicken breasts, or drumsticks can be used here instead of boneless chicken thighs.

PER SERVING **CALORIES: 335; SATURATED FAT: 2G; TOTAL FAT: 16G; PROTEIN: 44G; TOTAL CARBS: 9G; FIBER: 1G; SODIUM: 173MG**

Sausage and Asparagus Sheet Pan Dinner

SERVES
4 TO 6

PREP TIME:
10 MINUTES

COOK TIME:
30 MINUTES

DAIRY-FREE

GF

GLUTEN-FREE

This savory medley of crispy asparagus, cauliflower, and sausage is truly a one-pan wonder. At my house, we love to serve ours with lots of Dijon mustard and sauerkraut.

1 red onion, sliced

1 shallot, sliced

1 bunch (1½ to 2 pounds) asparagus, ends removed

1 head cauliflower, stemmed and cut

8 to 12 small pork sausages

Salt

Freshly ground black pepper

3 tablespoons extra-virgin olive oil

1. Preheat the oven to 450°F.

2. Line a large sheet pan with parchment paper (or aluminum foil).

3. Distribute the red onions, shallots, asparagus, cauliflower, and sausages evenly across the sheet pan. Season with salt and black pepper, and drizzle the oil over the entire pan.

4. Bake for 30 minutes, until the veggies are tender and golden brown and the sausages are fully cooked, or have reached an internal temperature of 160°F.

5. Serve immediately. Leftovers can be refrigerated in an airtight container up to four days.

Easy Substitution: For a heartier variation, switch out the asparagus and cauliflower for broccoli, Brussels sprouts, and red pepper.

PER SERVING CALORIES: 294; SATURATED FAT: 7G; TOTAL FAT: 25G; PROTEIN: 11G; TOTAL CARBS: 9G; FIBER: 3G; SODIUM: 1006MG

Easy Baked Ziti

Who doesn't love hot, cheese-filled pasta bundled in marinara sauce? This Italian restaurant classic is destined to become a family favorite, and probably requires less time in the kitchen than you think. Perfect for warming up those chilly nights, this dish is the ideal comfort food. You can freeze leftovers in a freezer-friendly container up to three months.

SERVES
4 TO 6

PREP TIME:
5 MINUTES

COOK TIME:
45 MINUTES

FREEZER-FRIENDLY

VEGETARIAN

2 (16-ounce) packages ziti pasta

2 (32-ounce) jars marinara

1 (8-ounce) package fresh mozzarella, sliced

2 tablespoons chopped fresh basil

1. Preheat the oven to 350°F.
2. Add the pasta to a large pot of boiling water and cook according to the package instructions until al dente (still firm), about 10 to 12 minutes. Drain and move to an oven-safe baking dish.
3. Toss the marinara through the pasta until well coated.
4. Layer the sliced mozzarella and basil over the pasta.
5. Bake 30 minutes, until the cheese bubbles.
6. Serve immediately. Leftovers can be refrigerated in an airtight container up to four days.

Lunch Remix: This recipe can be jazzed up for a next-day lunch or dinner by adding ground beef, sausage, or fresh spinach.

PER SERVING CALORIES: 724; SATURATED FAT: 5G; TOTAL FAT: 10G; PROTEIN: 29G; TOTAL CARBS: 124G; FIBER: 8G; SODIUM: 1758MG

Turkey Meatballs in Marinara

SERVES
4

PREP TIME:
15 MINUTES

COOK TIME:
35 MINUTES

FREEZER-
FRIENDLY

GF

GLUTEN-FREE

This recipe allows you to approximate a slow-cooked meal without spending hours in the kitchen. The meatballs are moist, tender, and packed with flavor. Put this one in permanent rotation—and don't forget the spaghetti! These will keep in a freezer-friendly container up to three months in the freezer.

1 pound ground turkey

Pinch salt

Dash freshly ground black pepper

3 tablespoons Worcestershire sauce

1 egg, large

2 tablespoons minced fresh parsley, plus more for garnish

2 tablespoons extra-virgin olive oil

1 (32-ounce) jar marinara

¼ cup Kalamata olives (optional)

Parmesan, for garnish

1. Preheat the oven to 375°F.

2. In a large bowl, fully combine the turkey, salt, black pepper, Worcestershire sauce, egg, and 2 tablespoons of parsley, and form into 10 to 12 small meatballs.

3. In a large skillet, heat the oil over medium heat.

4. Add the meatballs and cook for about 5 minutes on each side, until browned.

5. Remove the browned meatballs from the skillet and space them evenly in an oven-safe baking dish. Add the marinara and olives (if using).

6. Bake at 375°F for 20 to 25 minutes, until the meatballs are cooked through and have reached an internal temperature of 160°F.

7. Garnish with fresh Parmesan and parsley.

8. Serve immediately. Leftovers can be refrigerated in an airtight container up to four days.

Lunch Remix: Tomorrow, serve these meatballs over a bed of steamed vegetables or the noodles of your choice. Or, if you're looking for something extra special, use them in a hearty meatball sandwich with marinara and cheese.

PER SERVING **CALORIES: 334; SATURATED FAT: 5G; TOTAL FAT: 19G; PROTEIN: 27G; TOTAL CARBS: 15G;FIBER: 4G; SODIUM: 1365MG**

Extra Zesty Turkey Meatloaf

SERVES
4

PREP TIME:
10 MINUTES

COOK TIME:
30 MINUTES

DAIRY-FREE

FREEZER-FRIENDLY

Disclaimer: This is not your typical meatloaf. I've taken this old school staple and revamped it with extra seasoning and Worcestershire sauce. When I make this meatloaf for my family, I like to serve it with extra ketchup and Garlic Mashed Potatoes (see page 103). I also like to double this recipe and freeze what I don't serve in a freezer-friendly container. The loaf will stay good up to three months.

1 pound ground turkey

½ onion, minced

1 tablespoon dried oregano

1 egg, large

½ cup bread crumbs

2 tablespoons ketchup

1 tablespoon Worcestershire sauce

Pinch salt

Dash freshly ground black pepper

1. Preheat the oven to 350°F.
2. In a medium bowl, mix by hand the ground turkey, onion, dried oregano, egg, bread crumbs, ketchup, Worcestershire sauce, salt, and black pepper, until well combined.
3. Pack the mixture into a well-greased 9-by-5-inch loaf pan.
4. Bake for 30 minutes, or until well done (firm, golden brown, and with no redness inside when sliced).
5. Serve immediately. Leftovers will store well in an airtight glass container in the refrigerator up to four days.

Lunch Remix: This dish is wonderful—cold or reheated—for next-day lunch or dinner between two slices of your favorite sandwich bread, or over a bed of salad greens.

PER SERVING CALORIES: 258; SATURATED FAT: 3G; TOTAL FAT: 11G; PROTEIN: 23G; TOTAL CARBS: 15G; FIBER: 1G; SODIUM: 385MG

Spice-Rubbed Pork Tenderloin

The warm sweetness of cinnamon and maple syrup tinged with smoky chili powder gives this already tender pork tenderloin a distinctive flair. This dish is especially delicious served alongside a heap of Garlic Mashed Potatoes (see page 103). For a special treat, you can also pair this pork with roasted jalapeños.

SERVES
4 TO 6

PREP TIME:
10 MINUTES

COOK TIME:
35 MINUTES,
PLUS 5 MINUTES
TO REST

GF

GLUTEN-FREE

1 (1-pound) pork tenderloin

1 tablespoon ground cinnamon

1 tablespoon chili powder

1 teaspoon salt

Dash freshly ground black pepper

2 tablespoons unsalted butter

2 garlic cloves, minced

3 tablespoons real maple syrup

1. Preheat the oven to 350°F.

2. Rub the pork tenderloin thoroughly with cinnamon, chili powder, salt, and black pepper, then set aside.

3. In a large skillet, heat the butter over medium heat until melted.

4. Add the tenderloin, and brown for 2 to 3 minutes on each side.

5. Place the tenderloin in an oven-safe baking dish, and top with the garlic and maple syrup. Bake for 25 minutes, or until the internal temperature reaches 145°.

6. Remove from the oven and allow the tenderloin to rest for 5 minutes before slicing.

7. Serve immediately. Leftovers can be refrigerated in an airtight container up to four days.

Lunch Remix: This dish will reheat nicely for a next-day lunch or dinner, particularly sliced over a side salad or rice.

PER SERVING CALORIES: 222; SATURATED FAT: 5G; TOTAL FAT: 10G; PROTEIN: 21G; TOTAL CARBS: 13G; FIBER: 2G; SODIUM: 708MG

CHAPTER 6

Slow Cooker & Pressure Cooker

A slow cooker, as the name suggests, cooks your food slowly. A pressure cooker, on the other hand, cooks your food quickly. The operative word is "cooks"—as in, you don't actually have to do any of the cooking yourself. All you have to do is prep your favorite meat, vegetables, sauces, or stocks, throw them in the cooker and let these appliances do their thing. Refer to page 6 if you'd like to try making these recipes in the oven or on the stove, and check out the recipe tips for converting slow cooker recipes to pressure cooker recipes, and vice versa.

‹ Hearty Vegetarian Stew, page 76

Hearty Vegetarian Stew

SERVES
4 TO 6

PREP TIME:
15 MINUTES

COOK TIME:
45 MINUTES,
PLUS 1 MINUTE
TO REST

DAIRY-FREE

FREEZER-
FRIENDLY

GF

GLUTEN-FREE

VEGETARIAN

This robust, stick-to-your-ribs stew warms up the entire family. Serve as is, or with all the fixings: fresh cilantro, hot sauces, avocado slices, Cheddar cheese, sour cream, and jalapeños. If you have a high-speed blender, remove 2 cups of the finished soup, blend it, and return it to the stew for a creamier texture. The stew will last up to three months in a freezer-friendly container.

2 tablespoons extra-virgin olive oil

1 white onion, minced

3 garlic cloves, minced

2 thyme sprigs or 1 teaspoon dried thyme

Pinch salt

Dash freshly ground black pepper

3 cups dried kidney beans (presoaking unnecessary)

1 large tomato, cored and diced

1 red bell pepper, seeded and diced

1 tablespoon yellow mustard

1½ tablespoons ground cumin

2 tablespoons minced fresh cilantro

2 bay leaves

8 cups vegetable stock

1 (6-ounce) can tomato paste

1. Set the pressure cooker to sauté mode and heat the oil for 2 minutes, or until hot.

2. Add the onion, garlic, thyme, salt, and black pepper and sauté for 5 minutes, then turn off.

3. Add the beans, tomato, red pepper, mustard, cumin, cilantro, bay leaves, stock, and tomato paste, and place the lid on the pressure cooker.

4. Set the pressure cooker to manual (or high) and cook for 35 minutes. Once done, wait 1 minute, and release the pressure.

5. Serve immediately. Leftovers will store well in an airtight glass container in the refrigerator up to five days.

Make It Slower: If you are using a slow cooker with a sauté (or brown or sear) setting, perform steps 1 through 3 the same way, before adding the remaining ingredients and cooking everything on high for 4 hours. (Alternatively, you can sauté the onion, garlic, thyme, salt, and black pepper in the oil in a skillet over medium-high heat, before adding this mixture to the cooker.)

PER SERVING CALORIES: 623; SATURATED FAT: 1G; TOTAL FAT: 10G; PROTEIN: 35G; TOTAL CARBS: 105G; FIBER: 25G; SODIUM: 1008MG

Pressure Cooker Turkey Taco Bowls

SERVES
4 TO 6

PREP TIME:
10 MINUTES

COOK TIME:
35 MINUTES,
PLUS 5 MINUTES
TO REST

DAIRY-FREE

GF

GLUTEN-FREE

Here's an easy-to-make, one-pot meal packed with fresh, healthy ingredients to satisfy your desire for Mexican food. Serve as is or with Cheddar cheese, sour cream, lime wedges, or salsa, or combination of the four. Making this dish for vegetarians? No problem—simply omit the ground turkey and serve instead with avocado slices or Easy Guacamole (see page 96).

2 tablespoons extra-virgin olive oil

1 medium onion, diced

2 garlic cloves, diced

Pinch salt

Dash freshly ground black pepper

1 teaspoon chili powder

1 teaspoon ground cumin

1 pound ground turkey, crumbled

1 (15-ounce) can black beans, drained

1 cup sweet corn, fresh or frozen

1 cup white rice

1 (26-ounce) jar mild salsa

1 cup water

1. Set the pressure cooker to sauté mode and heat the oil for 2 minutes, or until hot.

2. Add the onion, garlic, salt, and black pepper and sauté for 5 minutes, then turn off.

3. Add the chili powder, cumin, ground turkey, beans, corn, rice, salsa, and water.

4. Set the pressure cooker to manual (or high) and cook for 30 minutes. Once done, wait 5 minutes, and release the pressure.

5. Serve immediately. Leftovers can be refrigerated in an airtight container up to four days.

Make It Slower: If you are using a slow cooker with a sauté (or brown or sear) setting, perform steps 1 and 2 the same way, before adding the remaining ingredients and cooking everything on high for 4 hours. (Alternatively, you can sauté the onion, garlic, salt, and black pepper in oil in a skillet on the stove, before adding this mixture to the cooker.)

PER SERVING **CALORIES: 583; SATURATED FAT: 4G; TOTAL FAT: 18G; PROTEIN: 33G; TOTAL CARBS: 72G; FIBER: 9G; SODIUM: 1161MG**

Pressure Cooker Smoked Paprika Chicken

SERVES
4

PREP TIME:
10 MINUTES

COOK TIME:
40 MINUTES,
PLUS 1 MINUTE
TO REST

DAIRY-FREE

FREEZER-
FRIENDLY

GF

GLUTEN-FREE

Braising the chicken in this rich, savory tomato sauce with smoky paprika makes for an effortless gourmet meal. My family prefers spooning this chicken over white rice. Store any leftovers in a freezer-friendly container up to three months.

2 tablespoons extra-virgin olive oil

1 onion, minced

2 garlic cloves, minced

8 bone-in chicken thighs

1 (32-ounce) jar marinara

1 teaspoon salt

Dash freshly ground black pepper

1 teaspoon smoked paprika

½ teaspoon dried thyme

2 cups water

1. Set the pressure cooker to sauté mode and heat the oil for 2 minutes, or until hot.

2. Add the onions and garlic, and sauté for 5 minutes, or until the onions are translucent, then turn off.

3. Add the chicken thighs, marinara, salt, black pepper, paprika, thyme, and water.

4. Set the pressure cooker to manual (or high) and cook for 30 minutes. Once done, wait 1 minute, and release the pressure.

5. Serve immediately. Leftovers can be refrigerated in an airtight container up to four days.

Make It Slower: If you are using a slow cooker with a sauté (or brown or sear) setting, perform steps 1 and 2, before adding the remaining ingredients and cooking everything on high for 4 hours. (Alternatively, you can sauté the onion and garlic in the oil in a skillet over medium-high heat, before adding these aromatics to the cooker.)

PER SERVING CALORIES: 489; SATURATED FAT: 9G; TOTAL FAT: 33G; PROTEIN: 34G; TOTAL CARBS: 16G; FIBER: 4G; SODIUM: 1543MG

Whole Slow Cooker Chicken

Set up this recipe in the slow cooker in the morning and you'll come home to the tantalizing smells of roasted chicken. The butternut squash will absorb the meat's delicious juices. (For a real feast, pair the chicken with the Garlic Mashed Potatoes [see page 103] or Simple Sweet Potato Fries [see page 104].)

SERVES
4 TO 6

PREP TIME:
10 MINUTES

COOK TIME:
4 HOURS

DAIRY-FREE

GF

GLUTEN-FREE

1 (10-ounce) bag frozen butternut squash

1 whole chicken

3 garlic cloves, minced

1 onion, sliced

1 orange, sliced

1 teaspoon salt

Dash freshly ground black pepper

1 tablespoon dried oregano

1 tablespoon dried thyme

1. Arrange the butternut squash on the bottom of your slow cooker, and place the whole chicken on top.

2. Place the garlic, onion, and orange around the chicken. Sprinkle the salt, black pepper, oregano, and thyme over the chicken.

3. Cover and set on high heat to cook for 4 hours.

4. Serve immediately. Leftovers can be refrigerated in an airtight container up to four days.

Lunch Remix: Pick the chicken and make an amazing chicken salad (like the Flatbread Chicken Salad Sandwiches on page 36) or shred the leftover chicken to pile high on simple salads.

Make It Faster: If you do not have a slow cooker, you can also make this recipe in a pressure cooker by simply adding all the ingredients and cooking on the manual (or high) setting for 35 minutes. Let the food rest for 1 minute, and release the pressure.

PER SERVING CALORIES: 388; SATURATED FAT: 6G; TOTAL FAT: 21G; PROTEIN: 32G; TOTAL CARBS: 18G; FIBER: 4G; SODIUM: 721MG

Sesame-Ginger Slow Cooker Chicken

SERVES
4

PREP TIME:
10 MINUTES

COOK TIME:
4 HOURS

DAIRY-FREE

GF
GLUTEN-FREE

This mouthwatering Asian-inspired dish encapsulates one of my favorite flavor combinations: sweet honey and salty soy sauce. I love to serve mine over white rice for a true, takeout-style dinner, or shred the leftover chicken and repurpose it for a chicken salad the next day.

8 bone-in chicken thighs

3 garlic cloves, sliced

1 tablespoon grated fresh ginger

3 tablespoons honey

1 cup soy sauce

2 tablespoons sesame oil

Pinch salt

Dash freshly ground black pepper

1. In a slow cooker, put in the chicken thighs, garlic, fresh ginger, honey, soy sauce, sesame oil, salt, and black pepper.

2. Close the lid, and cook on high for 4 hours.

3. Serve immediately. Leftovers can be refrigerated in an airtight container up to four days.

Make It Faster: If you're using a pressure cooker instead of a slow cooker, place all the ingredients as shown in step 1, then simply set to manual (or high) and cook for 35 minutes. Let the food rest for 1 minute, and release the pressure. Serve and enjoy.

PER SERVING CALORIES: 510; SATURATED FAT: 9G; TOTAL FAT: 32G; PROTEIN: 34G; TOTAL CARBS: 20G; FIBER: 1G; SODIUM: 3761MG

Slow Cooker Coconut Chicken

Lime, honey, and coconut milk guarantee this tender chicken will be full of flavor. I think this chicken is best served over rice, but if you're reheating it for tomorrow's lunch, you could put it over some steamed vegetables or pair it with a salad. Any extra can be frozen in a freezer-friendly container up to three months.

SERVES
4

PREP TIME:
10 MINUTES

COOK TIME:
4 HOURS

DAIRY-FREE

FREEZER-FRIENDLY

- **2 tablespoons extra-virgin olive oil**
- **1 onion, minced**
- **1 tablespoon fresh ginger, minced**
- **3 garlic cloves, minced**
- **3 tablespoons fresh cilantro, minced**
- **Pinch salt**
- **Dash freshly ground black pepper**
- **8 bone-in chicken thighs**
- **3 tablespoons fish sauce**
- **Juice of 1 lime**
- **½ cup soy sauce**
- **2 tablespoons honey**
- **1 (13.5-ounce) can full-fat coconut milk**

1. Set the slow cooker to sauté (or sear or brown) mode and heat the oil for 2 minutes, or until hot.

2. Add the onions, ginger, garlic, cilantro, salt, and black pepper, and sauté for 5 minutes, or until the onions are translucent, then turn off.

3. Add the chicken, fish sauce, lime juice, soy sauce, honey, and coconut milk. Cook on high for 4 hours.

4. Serve immediately. Leftovers can be refrigerated in an airtight container up to four days.

continued

Slow Cooker Coconut Chicken, continued

Make It Faster: Set the pressure cooker to sauté mode for 2 minutes, or until hot. Add the oil, onions, ginger, garlic, cilantro, salt, and black pepper, and sauté for 5 minutes, or until the onions are translucent, then turn off. Add the chicken, fish sauce, lime juice, soy sauce, honey, and coconut milk. Set the pressure cooker to manual (or high) and cook for 30 minutes. Let the food rest for 1 minute, and release the pressure.

Troubleshooting: If your slow cooker doesn't have a sauté (or brown or sear) setting, you can sauté the onion, ginger, garlic, cilantro, salt, and black pepper in the oil in a skillet over medium-high heat, before adding this mixture to the slow cooker.

PER SERVING **CALORIES: 678; SATURATED FAT: 26G; TOTAL FAT: 52G; PROTEIN: 35G; TOTAL CARBS: 19G; FIBER: 1G; SODIUM: 2521MG**

Pressure Cooker Sausage and Cabbage

Braising the cabbage and sauerkraut in your pressure cooker makes the cabbage wonderfully sweet and the Italian sausage incredibly tender—absolutely perfect on a busy weeknight. I like to serve this dish with some Garlic Mashed Potatoes (see page 103), as well as a good Dijon mustard for dipping.

SERVES
4 TO 6

PREP TIME:
10 MINUTES

COOK TIME:
30 MINUTES,
PLUS 1 MINUTE
TO REST

DAIRY-FREE

GF

GLUTEN-FREE

6 to 8 sweet Italian sausages

1 large green cabbage, core removed and chopped

1 (15-ounce) jar sauerkraut

1 (32-ounce) container low-sodium chicken stock

Pinch salt

Dash freshly ground black pepper

1. Put the sausages, cabbage, sauerkraut (with the juices), stock, salt, and black pepper in the pressure cooker, set to manual (or high), and cook for 30 minutes. Once done, wait 1 minute, and release the pressure.

2. Serve immediately. Leftovers can be refrigerated in an airtight container up to four days.

Lunch Remix: Leftovers can be reused the next day for lunches and dinners by tossing through your favorite pasta. You can make a slightly modified version of a classic kraut-and-kielbasa sandwich on a sub roll, too.

Make It Slower: If you don't have a pressure cooker, feel free to use a slow cooker. Just put all of the above ingredients in your slow cooker and set on high heat for 4 hours.

PER SERVING **CALORIES: 291; SATURATED FAT: 4G; TOTAL FAT: 11G; PROTEIN: 26G; TOTAL CARBS: 25G; FIBER: 11G; SODIUM: 1651MG**

Pressure Cooker
New Orleans Jambalaya

SERVES
4 TO 6

PREP TIME:
15 MINUTES

COOK TIME:
1 HOUR PLUS
1 MINUTE TO
REST

DAIRY-FREE

GF
GLUTEN-FREE

This popular New Orleans–style dish is a beautiful fusion of African, French, and Spanish cuisines. The bold, zesty flavors from the aromatics combine with the sausage and tomato sauce. And Jambalaya works just as well without the meat, so don't feel like you need to include the sausage.

2 tablespoons extra-virgin olive oil

1 medium onion, minced

3 garlic cloves, minced

1 green pepper, seeded and diced

3 celery stalks, minced

2 tablespoons minced fresh parsley

Pinch salt

Dash freshly ground black pepper

2 thyme sprigs

5 mild Italian sausages, removed from casings and chopped

1 (32-ounce) jar marinara

2 cups water

2½ cups uncooked white rice

1. Set the pressure cooker to sauté and heat the oil for 2 minutes, or until hot.

2. Add the onions, garlic, green pepper, celery, parsley, salt, black pepper, and thyme. Sauté for 5 minutes, or until the onions become translucent. Then add the sausages and sauté them for 5 minutes, until they begin to brown.

3. Turn off the pressure cooker, then add the marinara sauce, water, and rice.

4. Set the pressure cooker to manual (or high). Cook for 45 minutes. Let the food rest for 1 minute, and release the pressure.

5. Serve immediately. Leftovers can be refrigerated in an airtight container up to four days.

Lunch Remix: For a tasty brunch, add a fried egg and hot sauce to the reheated leftovers.

Make It Slower: If you are using a slow cooker with a sauté (or brown or sear) setting, perform steps 1 and 2 the same way. Then add the remaining ingredients and cook everything on high for 4 hours. (Alternatively, you can sauté the onion, garlic, green pepper, celery, parsley, salt, black pepper, thyme, and sausage in the oil in a skillet over medium-high heat, before adding this mixture to the cooker.)

PER SERVING **CALORIES: 615; SATURATED FAT: 3G; TOTAL FAT: 13G; PROTEIN: 15G; TOTAL CARBS: 110G; FIBER: 6G; SODIUM: 1368MG**

Easy Beef Bolognese

SERVES
4 TO 6

PREP TIME:
10 MINUTES

COOK TIME:
4 HOURS
10 MINUTES

DAIRY-FREE

FREEZER-
FRIENDLY

You're likely quite familiar with Bolognese, that classic Italian meat-based pasta sauce. Now you can make this staple at home—and with ease. Children and adults alike will be unable to resist a soul-satisfying heaping of pasta smothered in ground beef and a hearty tomato sauce. Don't forget to make extra: This Bolognese keeps surprisingly well in the freezer up to three months.

2 tablespoons extra-virgin olive oil

1 onion, minced

2 garlic cloves, minced

Pinch salt

Dash freshly ground black pepper

1 tablespoon dried oregano

1 pound ground beef

1 (10-ounce) bag frozen spinach (optional)

1 (24-ounce) jar marinara

1 cup water

1 pound penne noodles

1. Set the slow cooker to sauté (or sear or brown) mode for 2 minutes, or until hot.

2. Sauté the oil, onion, garlic, salt, black pepper, and oregano for 2 minutes.

3. Add the ground beef and continue to sauté for another 5 minutes.

4. Add the frozen spinach (if using), marinara, and water, and cook on high for 3 hours.

5. Add the noodles, and cook on high for 1 hour.

6. Serve immediately.

Make It Faster: Set the pressure cooker to sauté mode for 2 minutes, or until hot. Add the oil, onion, garlic, salt, black pepper, and oregano and sauté for 5 minutes, then turn off. Add the ground beef, frozen spinach (if using), marinara, and water. Set the pressure cooker to manual (or high) and cook for 30 minutes. Add the penne and seal the cooker for 5 more minutes. Let the food rest for 1 minute before releasing the pressure and serving.

Troubleshooting: If your slow cooker doesn't have a sauté (or brown or sear) setting, you can sauté the onion, garlic, salt, black pepper, oregano, and ground beef in the oil in a skillet over medium-high heat, before putting this mixture in the slow cooker with the remaining ingredients.

PER SERVING **CALORIES: 564; SATURATED FAT: 8G; TOTAL FAT: 24G; PROTEIN: 23G; TOTAL CARBS: 62G; FIBER: 3G; SODIUM: 665MG**

Red Wine–Braised Beef

SERVES
4 TO 6

PREP TIME:
15 MINUTES

COOK TIME:
45 MINUTES,
PLUS 1 MINUTE
TO REST

DAIRY-FREE

FREEZER-
FRIENDLY

GF

GLUTEN-FREE

Serve this wine-braised beef to your dinner guests, and you'll have them wondering whether you've slaved away in the kitchen all day. The answer, of course, will be "no." This dish is the ultimate comfort food for any busy night and is delicious on its own, or spooned over some lightly buttered noodles. Feel free to make extra to freeze in a freezer-friendly container up to three months.

2 tablespoons extra-virgin olive oil

2 celery stalks, ends removed and chopped

4 carrots, peeled and chopped

1 white onion, minced

3 garlic cloves, minced

Pinch salt

Dash freshly ground black pepper

2 tablespoons minced fresh parsley

3 thyme sprigs

5 potatoes, sliced

1 (7-ounce) tomato paste

3 bay leaves (optional)

1 pound beef chuck roast

1 cup red wine

1 cup low-sodium beef broth

1. Set the pressure cooker to sauté mode for 2 minutes, or until hot.

2. Sauté the oil, celery, carrots, onion, garlic, salt, black pepper, parsley, and thyme for 5 minutes.

3. Add the potatoes, tomato paste, bay leaves (if using), chuck roast, wine, and beef broth.

4. Set the pressure cooker to manual (or high) and cook for 35 minutes. Once done, wait 1 minute, and release the pressure.

5. Remove the roast, slice, and put back in the pressure cooker.

6. Serve from the pressure cooker. Leftovers can be refrigerated in an airtight container up to four days.

Make It Slower: If you are using a slow cooker with a sauté (or brown or sear) setting, perform steps 1 and 2 in the same way. Then add the potatoes, tomato paste, bay leaves (if using), chuck roast, wine, and beef broth, and cook everything on high for 4 hours. (Alternatively, you can sauté the celery, carrots, onion, garlic, salt, black pepper, parsley, and thyme in the oil in a small skillet over medium-high heat, before adding this mixture to the slow cooker.)

PER SERVING **CALORIES: 449; SATURATED FAT: 1G; TOTAL FAT: 14G; PROTEIN: 30G; TOTAL CARBS: 52G; FIBER: 9G; SODIUM: 106MG**

CHAPTER 7

Simple Sides

As the title of this chapter suggests, all of these tantalizing sides—from the Simple Sweet Potato Fries (see page 104), to the Tomato and Caper Pasta Salad (see page 99)—can be made in just three steps. Feel free to mix and match these dishes with this book's entrées.

How to Refresh Your Classic Sides

There are so many ways to easily refresh classic side dishes to make them more interesting and delicious. Here are a handful of my favorites.

- Simple **white rice** can be freshened up by cooking or steaming in low-sodium chicken or vegetable stock. Also, adding a pat of butter or a drizzle of olive oil is an easy, quick way to give rice a greater depth of flavor.

- **Mashed potatoes** can be made more interesting by adding fresh herbs, or mashing the potatoes with buttermilk or fresh garlic, or all three.

- Adding a squeeze of lemon or lime juice to a **side salad** along with fresh herbs, like cilantro, fresh basil, and parsley, is a great way to jazz up no-cook lunches.

- You can make healthy **lentils, chickpeas, and quinoa** more interesting if you add a teaspoon of ground cumin or chili powder.

- Enhance **roasted potatoes** with a combination of dried oregano, ground cumin, chili powder, or minced garlic.

- Squeeze the juice of a slice of lemon or lime over your **steamed or roasted vegetables** for added flavor.

- You can quick-pickle **raw, sliced veggies** of any kind by placing them in a small bowl with ½ cup apple cider vinegar, 1 teaspoon sea salt, and 2 tablespoons real maple syrup.

Chef Emery's Famous Cranberry Sauce

Few of my recipes have received as elated a reception from friends and family as this one. Not only will this sauce be your go-to for special occasions and holidays, it will liven up any ol' meal. The combination of citrus spiked with cinnamon and notes of nutmeg really brings out the best in the tart cranberries. Serve with roast chicken, turkey, and pork, or let it add some extra flair to your cheese board!

SERVES
4 TO 6

PREP TIME:
10 MINUTES

COOK TIME:
35 MINUTES

DAIRY-FREE

GF

GLUTEN-FREE

VEGETARIAN

Zest of 1 lemon (about 1 tablespoon)

Zest of 1 orange (about 1½ tablespoons)

Pinch salt

1 teaspoon cinnamon

1 teaspoon grated fresh nutmeg

1½ cups sugar

1½ cups water

1 (8-ounce) package cranberries

1. In a medium saucepan, heat the lemon zest, orange zest, salt, cinnamon, nutmeg, sugar, water, and cranberries over high heat until boiling.

2. Boil for 30 minutes or until the liquid reduces by about half and the sauce is nice and thick.

3. Let cool, then serve or refrigerate in an airtight glass container up to 7 to 10 days.

Lunch Remix: This dish can accompany many recipes, but also makes a fantastic spread for your favorite sandwich—especially turkey.

PER SERVING CALORIES: 211; SATURATED FAT: 0G; TOTAL FAT: 0G; PROTEIN: 0G; TOTAL CARBS: 54G; FIBER: 2G; SODIUM: 27MG

Easy Guacamole

DAIRY-FREE

GF

GLUTEN-FREE

VEGETARIAN

30-MINUTE

If you're like me, you could probably eat your body weight in guacamole. I love the rich and buttery, yet playfully acidic, combination of flavors. Go ahead and add this side to any of the Mexican-inspired mains throughout this book. Or grab a bag of tortilla chips and eat a batch on its own.

3 avocados, pits removed and flesh scooped out

2 tablespoons onion, minced

Juice of 1 lime

Pinch salt

Dash freshly ground black pepper

1. In a medium bowl, mash the avocado with a fork and combine with the onion, lime juice, salt, and black pepper until the texture is smooth.

2. Serve immediately and enjoy.

Pair With: The options are endless, but I often love guacamole on toast with eggs of any kind.

PER SERVING **CALORIES: 221; SATURATED FAT: 3G; TOTAL FAT: 20G; PROTEIN: 3G; TOTAL CARBS: 13G; FIBER: 9G; SODIUM: 50MG**

Quick-Pickled Cucumbers

With this recipe, you're only minutes away from an explosion of flavor. The cucumbers absorb all the sharpness of the salty vinegar, while still leaving a hint of sweetness from the maple syrup. Feel free to store this dish in an airtight container in the refrigerator up to six days. In fact, the cucumbers will just get better and better the longer they marinate.

4 cucumbers, peeled and sliced
½ cup apple cider vinegar
2 tablespoons real maple syrup

Pinch salt
Freshly ground black pepper

1. In a medium bowl, fully combine the cucumbers, vinegar, maple syrup, salt, and black pepper.
2. Let the cucumbers marinate on the counter or in the refrigerator for 20 minutes before serving.

Pair With: These cucumbers will jazz up any sandwich. They also make a perfect topping on almost any kind of salad!

PER SERVING **CALORIES: 78; SATURATED FAT: 0G; TOTAL FAT: 0G; PROTEIN: 2G; TOTAL CARBS: 18G; FIBER: 2G; SODIUM: 47MG**

SERVES
4 TO 6

PREP TIME:
5 MINUTES

MARINATE TIME:
20 MINUTES

DAIRY-FREE

GF
GLUTEN-FREE

VEGETARIAN

30-MINUTE

Lemon Quinoa Salad

SERVES
4 TO 6

PREP TIME:
15 MINUTES

COOK TIME:
20 MINUTES

DAIRY-FREE

GF

GLUTEN-FREE

VEGETARIAN

With the combination of crunchy veggies, robust herbs, and lemony dressing, this healthy salad just can't be beat. Great for a potluck, barbecue, or light lunch, this side complements almost anything. Feel free to make extra and store in an airtight container in your refrigerator up to five days.

2 cups quinoa

2 cups water

½ red pepper, seeded and diced

½ yellow pepper, seeded and diced

1 cup black olives, pitted and sliced

2 tablespoons minced fresh mint

2 tablespoons minced fresh cilantro

Juice of 1 lemon

1 teaspoon salt

Dash freshly ground black pepper

1 cup Italian vinaigrette

1. In a medium saucepan, bring the quinoa and water to a boil. Reduce the heat to low, cover, and cook for 20 minutes, or until tender.

2. In a medium bowl, toss to combine the cooked quinoa, red peppers, yellow peppers, olives, mint, cilantro, lemon juice, salt, and black pepper, and vinaigrette. Serve immediately.

Easy Substitution: The red and yellow peppers can be swapped out for any crunchy vegetable you love, like broccoli. You can also replace some of the herbs with fresh basil.

PER SERVING **CALORIES: 424; SATURATED FAT: 3G; TOTAL FAT: 21G; PROTEIN: 9G; TOTAL CARBS: 53G; FIBER: 5G; SODIUM: 1211MG**

Tomato and Caper Pasta Salad

Juicy tomatoes paired with fresh capers and lemon—the ideal flavor combination for a light, bright summer pasta salad. Grill something up and serve this dish as a side, or make as the main dish and serve with a big salad.

SERVES
4 TO 6

PREP TIME:
10 MINUTES

COOK TIME:
15 MINUTES

1 (16-ounce) package rotini pasta

½ cup mayonnaise

½ (2-ounce) jar capers

Juice of 1 lemon

1 teaspoon dried oregano

3 celery stalks, chopped

½ pint cherry tomatoes, halved

2 tablespoons minced fresh parsley

1 teaspoon salt

Dash freshly ground black pepper

DAIRY-FREE

VEGETARIAN

30-MINUTE

1. Add the pasta to a large pot of boiling water and cook according to the package instructions until al dente (still firm), about 10 to 12 minutes. Drain and set aside to cool.

2. In a large bowl, fully combine the mayonnaise, capers (with their juices), lemon juice, oregano, celery, tomatoes, parsley, salt, and black pepper.

3. Add the cooked pasta and toss well, then serve immediately.

Pair With: This side is fantastic for Turkey Burgers with Caramelized Onions (see page 55) or the Honey Mustard Glazed Sheet Pan Chicken (see page 67).

PER SERVING CALORIES: 352; SATURATED FAT: 1G; TOTAL FAT: 8G; PROTEIN: 10G; TOTAL CARBS: 62G; FIBER: 4G; SODIUM: 676MG

Mediterranean Potato Salad

SERVES
4 TO 6

PREP TIME:
10 MINUTES

COOK TIME:
25 MINUTES

DAIRY-FREE

GF

GLUTEN-FREE

VEGETARIAN

I've been making a version of this potato salad since I was a little kid, and there's a reason. The creamy, fluffy potatoes tossed with lemon juice and olives will take your next cook-out (or any dinner, really) to the next level. Make a big batch and refrigerate in an airtight container up to five days, spooning out portions at mealtimes until it's gone (which won't take long).

6 large yellow potatoes, halved

3 tablespoons fresh parsley

½ cup mayonnaise

Juice of 1 lemon

1 (2-ounce) jar capers

1 cup pitted Kalamata olives, sliced

1 teaspoon salt, plus more to season

Dash freshly ground black pepper, plus more to season

1. Add the potatoes to a large pot three-quarters full of cold water over high heat and bring to a boil. Cook for 25 minutes, or until fork tender, then remove from the heat and drain.

2. In a large bowl, combine the parsley, mayonnaise, lemon juice, capers (with their juices), olives, salt, and black pepper.

3. Slice the potatoes into the bowl, toss well, and season with salt and black pepper. Serve immediately.

Pair With: Try this dish with Marinated Asian-Style Chicken (see page 40) or Sheet Pan Barbecue Chicken and Roasted Veggies (see page 65).

PER SERVING CALORIES: 382; SATURATED FAT: 1G; TOTAL FAT: 9G; PROTEIN: 8G; TOTAL CARBS: 71G; FIBER: 9G; SODIUM: 962MG

Cilantro Lime Rice

White rice by itself is great, but it's incredibly easy to make it *so* much better. This lime-spiked option with olive oil—a beautiful balance of acid and fat—is my favorite iteration. Especially good with any kind of Mexican food, this rice also pairs well with fish and shrimp.

2 cups water

Pinch salt

2 cups white rice

3 tablespoons minced fresh cilantro

Juice of 1 lime

3 tablespoons extra-virgin olive oil

SERVES
4 TO 6

PREP TIME:
5 MINUTES

COOK TIME:
30 MINUTES

DAIRY-FREE

GF

GLUTEN-FREE

VEGETARIAN

1. In a medium saucepan, bring the water and salt to a boil. Add the rice, reduce the heat to low and cover, cooking for 30 minutes or until the rice is tender and all the water is absorbed.

2. Add the cilantro, lime juice, and oil.

3. Stir well and serve immediately.

Troubleshooting: A rice cooker, if you have one, is the best way to make the rice. You can set it and forget it, and add the rest of the ingredients before serving.

PER SERVING **CALORIES: 431; SATURATED FAT: 2G; TOTAL FAT: 11G; PROTEIN: 7G; TOTAL CARBS: 75G; FIBER: 1G; SODIUM: 44MG**

Roasted Sheet Pan Veggies with Jalapeño

SERVES
4

PREP TIME:
10 MINUTES

COOK TIME:
30 MINUTES

DAIRY-FREE

GF

GLUTEN-FREE

VEGETARIAN

Of course, you could really throw any vegetables you have on hand onto a sheet pan, but the jalapeño is what really gives this side a spicy, unique flair. Serve this dish with rice and beans for a complete Mexican-inspired dinner, and store the leftovers in the refrigerator in an airtight container up to three days.

1 head broccoli, stemmed and chopped

1 shallot, sliced

2 summer squash, ends removed and sliced

2 zucchinis, ends removed and sliced

2 jalapeño peppers, seeded and sliced

Salt

Freshly ground black pepper

3 tablespoons extra-virgin olive oil

1. Preheat the oven to 450°F.

2. Lay the broccoli, shallots, squash, zucchinis, and jalapeños on a large, rimmed sheet pan. Season with salt and black pepper, then drizzle the oil evenly across the pan.

3. Bake for 30 minutes or until tender and golden brown. Serve immediately.

Lunch Remix: These roasted veggies can be served the next day over a simple green salad, cooked quinoa, or rice to make a complete meal. You can even add a fried egg.

PER SERVING CALORIES: 156; SATURATED FAT: 2G; TOTAL FAT: 11G; PROTEIN: 5G; TOTAL CARBS: 14G; FIBER: 5G; SODIUM: 89MG

Garlic Mashed Potatoes

A well-known chef taught me a quick trick for making superior garlic mashed potatoes—and once you've tried this version, you'll never make them another way, again. Buttery, creamy goodness is in perfect harmony with the garlic here. These potatoes will elevate almost any dinner, but go particularly well with meatloaf, pork tenderloin, and sausage and cabbage.

SERVES
4 TO 6

PREP TIME:
I5 MINUTES

COOK TIME:
25 MINUTES

GF
GLUTEN-FREE

VEGETARIAN

6 large yellow potatoes, peeled and quartered

3 garlic cloves, halved

1½ cups buttermilk

3 tablespoons unsalted butter

1 teaspoon salt

Dash freshly ground black pepper

1. Add the potatoes and garlic to a medium pot three-quarters full of cold water over high heat and bring to a boil. Cook for 25 minutes, or until fork tender, then remove from the heat and drain.

2. Return the potatoes and garlic to the pot and add the buttermilk, butter, salt, and black pepper, then mash well with a fork until smooth.

3. Serve immediately. Leftovers can be refrigerated in an airtight container up to four days.

Make It Faster: If you have an electric mixer, simply beat all the ingredients on medium until they're smoothly whipped.

PER SERVING **CALORIES: 337; SATURATED FAT: 6G; TOTAL FAT: 10G; PROTEIN: 9G; TOTAL CARBS: 55G; FIBER: 8G; SODIUM: 759MG**

Simple Sweet Potato Fries

SERVES
4

PREP TIME:
10 MINUTES

COOK TIME:
30 MINUTES

DAIRY-FREE

GF

GLUTEN-FREE

VEGETARIAN

Nothing beats a simple, healthy side that tastes like French fries. These crispy, salty fries, tinged with sweetness, are heaven on a plate. Serve them with burgers, roasts, and sandwiches. And here's a secret: They'll even work alongside your favorite egg dish for breakfast!

3 large sweet potatoes, peeled and sliced

3 tablespoons extra-virgin olive oil

Salt

Freshly ground black pepper

1. Preheat the oven to 450°F.

2. Lay the sweet potatoes on a large sheet pan. Drizzle the oil evenly over the potatoes, then season the whole pan with salt and black pepper.

3. Bake for 30 minutes, until crispy and golden brown. Serve and enjoy.

Pair With: The Extra Zesty Turkey Meatloaf (see page 72) and Spice-Rubbed Pork Tenderloin (see page 73) are perfect entrées to match with these sweet potato fries.

PER SERVING **CALORIES: 174; SATURATED FAT: 2G; TOTAL FAT: 11G; PROTEIN: 2G; TOTAL CARBS: 20G; FIBER: 3G; SODIUM: 92MG**

Measurement Conversions

Volume Equivalents (liquid)

Standard	U.S. Standard (ounces)	Metric (approximate)
2 tablespoons	1 fl. oz.	30 mL
¼ cup	2 fl. oz.	60 mL
½ cup	4 fl. oz.	120 mL
1 cup	8 fl. oz.	240 mL
1½ cups	12 fl. oz.	355 mL
2 cups or 1 pint	16 fl. oz.	475 mL
4 cups or 1 quart	32 fl. oz.	1 L
1 gallon	128 fl. oz.	4 L

Oven Temperatures

Fahrenheit (F)	Celsius (C) (approximate)
250°	120°
300°	150°
325°	165°
350°	180°
375°	190°
400°	200°
425°	220°
450°	230°

Volume Equivalents (dry)

Standard	Metric (approximate)
⅛ teaspoon	0.5 mL
¼ teaspoon	1 mL
½ teaspoon	2 mL
¾ teaspoon	4 mL
1 teaspoon	5 mL
1 tablespoon	15 mL
¼ cup	59 mL
⅓ cup	79 mL
½ cup	118 mL
⅔ cup	156 mL
¾ cup	177 mL
1 cup	235 mL
2 cups or 1 pint	475 mL
3 cups	700 mL
4 cups or 1 quart	1 L

Weight Equivalents

Standard	Metric (approximate)
½ ounce	15 g
1 ounce	30 g
2 ounces	60 g
4 ounces	115 g
8 ounces	225 g
12 ounces	340 g
16 ounces or 1 pound	455 g

References

Organisation for Economic Co-operation and Development (OECD). "Balancing Paid Work, Unpaid Work and Leisure." May 3, 2018. https://www.oecd.org /gender/balancing-paid-work-unpaid-work-and-leisure.htm.

Dewey, Caitlin. "Why You Should (Really, Seriously, Permanently) Stop Using Your Smartphone at Dinner." *The Washington Post*, July 14, 2014. https://www .washingtonpost.com/news/the-intersect/wp/2014/07/14/why-you-should-reall y-seriously-permanently-stop-using-your-smartphone-at-dinner/.

Dwyer, Ryan J., Kostadin Kushlev, and Elizabeth W. Dunn. "Smartphone Use Undermines Enjoyment of Face-to-Face Social Interactions." *Journal of Experimental Social Psychology* 78 (Sept. 2018): 233–39. https://doi.org/10.1016/j. jesp.2017.10.007.

United States Department of Agriculture. Economic Research Service. *Adult Eating and Health Patterns: Evidence From the 2014–16 Eating & Health Module of the American Time Use Survey*, by Eliana Zeballos and Brandon Restrepo. EIB-198. October 2018. https://www.ers.usda.gov/webdocs /publications/90466/eib-198.pdf?v=2608.6.

Index

Acknowledgments

A special thank you to my husband, Troy, and friends Kiki, Shan, Sarah, Beth, and Mary Frances, whose steadfast friendship and support always carries me through. Thank you for always believing in me.

About the Author

Chef Emery is a chef, food educator, cooking teacher, and mother, whose focus is on empowering wellness through real food. An expert at helping busy home cooks make easy, quick, and delicious meals, her larger mission is to illuminate the impact of food choices on our own health and the health of the planet. She is the author of *The Heartfelt Cookbook* and *Empowerful,* and she has contributed to *Organic Spa Magazine* and *Total Teen* with Rodale Kids publishing. Her work can be found at www.ChefEmery.com, and you can follow her on Instagram @chef_emery.

CPSIA information can be obtained
at www.ICGtesting.com
Printed in the USA
JSHW021727010320
4447JS00002B/2